Working Scientifically

With the changes that have taken place to the National Curriculum for science, the investigations that children should experience have broadened and become a key part of the curriculum necessary for the development of knowledge and understanding. *Working Scientifically* is a comprehensive guide that will help primary teachers develop their skills, improve their practice and nurture 'Working scientifically' in the classroom.

This guide provides teachers with some tools and resources that are necessary for teaching science in a fun and exploratory way. Focusing on individual skills, it provides scientific activities in a number of different contexts. It explores each skill multiple times to help pupils progress through the age-related expectations and emphasises teaching through exploration, questioning and dialogue.

Using the analogy of a journey to space as the central concept, with each step of progression related to a step in the journey, chapters include:

- What is 'Working scientifically'?
- Raising questions, predictions and planning
- Observations, measuring and recording
- Interpreting, analysing and concluding
- Reflecting and evaluating
- Assessment.

Full of practical resources such as planning materials and assessment sheets, *Working Scientifically* will be an essential guide for all qualified and trainee primary teachers wishing to develop their practice in this essential area of the science curriculum.

Kevin Smith has worked in science education for 26 years and is Assistant Head Teacher in a cross phase special school. He is also a Consultant and Lecturer on Primary Science Initial Teacher Training courses in a number of universities in London, UK.

Working Scientifically
A guide for primary science teachers

Kevin Smith

Routledge
Taylor & Francis Group

LONDON AND NEW YORK

First published 2016
by Routledge
2 Park Square, Milton Park, Abingdon, Oxon OX14 4RN

and by Routledge
711 Third Avenue, New York, NY 10017

Routledge is an imprint of the Taylor & Francis Group, an informa business

© 2016 Kevin Smith

British Library Cataloguing in Publication Data
A catalogue record for this book is available from the British Library

Library of Congress Cataloging in Publication Data
Names: Smith, Kevin, 1965- author.Title: Working scientifically : a guide for primary science teachers / Kevin Smith.Description: Abingdon, Oxon : New York, NY : Routledge, 2016. | Includes bibliographical references.Identifiers: LCCN 2015046132| ISBN 9781138121980 (hardback) | ISBN 9781138121997 (pbk.) | ISBN 9781315650661 (ebook)Subjects: LCSH: Science--Study and teaching (Primary)--Great Britain.Classification: LCC LB1585.5.G7 S65 2016 | DDC 372.35/044--dc23LC record available at http://lccn.loc.gov/2015046132

ISBN: 978-1-138-12198-0 (hbk)
ISBN: 978-1-138-12199-7 (pbk)
ISBN: 978-1-315-65066-1 (ebk)

Typeset in Helvetica
by Saxon Graphics Ltd, Derby

MIX
Paper from
responsible sources
FSC
www.fsc.org   FSC® C013604

Printed and bound by CPI Group (UK) Ltd, Croydon, CR0 4YY

Contents

Acknowledgements

Many thanks to:

- Claude Bonnaud, skilled artist and graphic designer (www.claudebonnaud.com).
- Rob Toplis, Alex Sinclair and Mick Allen, critical friends who challenged my assumptions, gave me guidance and led to a better publication.
- I am indebted to all the fantastic publications that are out there and the people I have worked with within the ASE and NAIGS, and indeed all the fabulous, hard-working teachers I have met in my travels. You have provided necessary experience and inspiration on my journey and each and every one of you has played a small part in this publication.
- Also to FX – my rock.

All illustrations copyright of Claude Bonnaud, with the exception of pages 30, 64, 162, 165–168, 175 (trilobite) and 176 copyright of Andrew Cameron, Karate Grafika Ltd.

Introduction

So, why this guide? There are plenty of publications out there, plenty of schemes of work and plenty of academic texts that you may remember or you may be using at the current time. Surely there isn't a need for *another* book on how to teach science?

There is! And my reasons for writing one are simple:

1   As a trainer of teachers I see many student teachers and new or inexperienced enthusiastic teachers who understand the value of practical work as an engaging activity that children love and are excited about, but haven't yet grasped the pivotal role that investigative work plays in progression within science. I want to help you understand that role so that a practical activity becomes meaningful for both you and the children you teach. As Ofsted (2013) note, 'For pupils to achieve well in science, they must not only acquire the necessary knowledge, but also understand its value, enjoy the experience of working scientifically, and sustain their interest in learning it.'

2   There seems to me to be a disconnect between the formalised training of teachers and practice in the classroom. On the one hand, we have Initial Teacher Training/Education routes delivering very relevant and meaningful training, which is essential for the teacher to understand how their children learn. On the other hand, the reality is that many teachers necessarily leave this theory, this academic world, at the door when it comes to practice. It becomes part of their fabric yet ultimately becomes 'lost' in the day-to-day life of a busy teacher. I want to help you bridge that gap.

3   The National Curriculum in England: Science programmes of study (DfE 2013 and subsequent updates 2015) has changed again (see Figure 0.1). This has implications for *all* primary teachers. First, for the progress of your pupils, and second for your development as a teacher able to deliver an effective broad and balanced curriculum. I want to help secure your understanding of this curriculum area and how the skills contained in the curriculum progress over the year groups.

This guide is primarily concerned with the part of the National Curriculum in England: Science programmes of study known as 'Working scientifically'. However, since it is best practice to contextualise this part of the curriculum all activities will explore aspects (old and new) of the new 2015 curriculum. It is not meant to be an academic piece of work nor is it meant to be a scheme of work. My intention is for this to be a companion guide for you, a sharing of and source of ideas (and a few techniques), and finally an exploration of a very topical issue, that of assessment in primary science.

So, who is this guide written for? This guide is primarily for teachers in training or who are right at the beginning of their career. However, I am aware that there are teachers out there with plenty of experience who are nonetheless confused with the changes in the National Curriculum or else want to consolidate their experiences thus far. If that is you, then it is for you, too!

- Seasonal changes new at KS1.
- Evolution and inheritance, fossil formation, digestion, the digestive system, gears, levers and pulleys in KS2.
- Sound, light and forces have been moved from KS1 to KS2.
- Greater emphasis on: identifying and classifying and naming plants and animals.
- Terminology of 'Working scientifically' now used to describe scientific processes.
- Increased range and scope of 'Working scientifically' to include more investigations than fair testing, including observing over time, identifying and classifying, seeking patterns, and researching using secondary sources in order to answer scientific questions.

Figure 0.1 Main changes in the primary science curriculum.

In conclusion what will this guide do? It will:

- introduce you to the changes in the National Curriculum in England: Science programmes of study and the age-related expectations (ARE)
- develop your understanding of progress within 'Working scientifically'
- develop your skills and confidence in 'Working scientifically' and show you how to develop them in context of the content from the new National Curriculum
- suggest a variety of investigations to develop the skills
- suggest some approaches to developing the children's skills
- provide an example of a mastery assessment scheme based on formative assessment that can be used as a starting point to develop your own assessment system.

It will not:

- tell you the definitive way to develop these skills
- tell you the definitive way to assess this area of the curriculum or how frequently to do it
- give you prescriptive lesson plans but provide enough structure for you to create, innovate and do what you do best.
- give you risk assessments for each practical activity. It is the responsibility for the teacher to carry out a full risk assessment before they carry out any practical activity with the children.

I hope you enjoy it and it proves useful to you.

1 What is 'Working scientifically'?

What is 'Working scientifically' and why bother teaching it?

It is true to say that investigative work has in the past not been given the same degree of emphasis as it currently has. The days of the occasional demonstration and the rigid, teacher-led practical activity seem to have gone. The fundamental shift of looking at the whole scientific process, its central role in developing theory and a justifiable emphasis on the 'importance of science' began when investigative science was developed as a curriculum area in the original National Curriculum for England in 1989 (I can remember this well as I was hastily given my first post of responsibility in my second year of teaching to deal with the seventeen attainment targets and 'AT1'), but gathered further momentum in the 1999 review and change. With subsequent changes to the National Curriculum over the years, the terminologies have changed, the range of skills broadened, and as a result 'Working scientifically' has increasingly taken a central role within the curriculum until we have arrived at our current set of definitions and terminologies used in the National Curriculum.

Precisely because of the many changes over the years, developing an understanding of 'Working scientifically' can be problematic. The understanding of this term is dependent on who you ask, what stage they are at in their career, when a text you read was written, what and who you read and what version of the curriculum you are using. Therefore, you could well see the following phrases/terminologies that are sometimes used interchangeably:

Sc1
AT1
Inquiry skills
Enquiry Skills
Scientific enquiry
Investigative work
How science works
Scientific investigations
Working scientifically.

Generally, if you see:

SC1/AT1/ Scientific Enquiry: this relates to the curriculum pre-2000.
How science works: this relates to the curriculum post-2000, pre-2014.
Working scientifically: this relates to the curriculum post-2013.

Something to also be aware of is where a text has been written, as the terminologies might be slightly different. For example, in the UK, inquiry and enquiry are interchangeable yet in the US 'inquiry' is used. (However, it is becoming preferable to use inquiry to denote an investigation, and enquiry to denote a question.) It also depends on what scheme your school might have.

For clarity we will use the terminologies associated with the National Curriculum of England (framework document) September 2013, and subsequent updates, in this guide.

The National Curriculum in England: Science programmes of study (2015) states that:

> Working scientifically specifies the understanding of the nature, processes and methods of science for each year group.
>
> National Curriculum in England: Science programmes of study

It then outlines the nature, processes and methods of science for each year (Figure 1.1). It further uses the phrase 'scientific enquiry' in its explanation and introduces the reader to a number of scientific enquiries which will be referred to later. It then details what should be taught (statutory) and gives some guidance (non-statutory). I would argue that to develop the teaching of 'Working scientifically' we need to do more than identify what skills it encompasses. We also need to tease apart those skills to gain an insight into what they might look like in the classroom to children and understand the steps in development of them all. Once we understand how each skill develops, we then need to recognise the practical activities, techniques and contexts that are effective for developing these skills, with the ultimate aim of helping children to becoming autonomous investigators.

Harlen and Qualter (2015: 98) help us by classifying the skills as:

- raising questions, predicting and planning (concerned with setting up investigations)
- gathering evidence by observing and using information sources (collecting data from investigations)
- analysing, interpreting and explaining evidence (making conclusions in investigations)
- communicating, arguing, reflecting and evaluating evidence (evaluating their investigations).

For some this is a very useful approach and in this guide I will use this as the basis for my chapters.

Key Stage 1 (Years 1 and 2)

- Ask simple questions and recognise they can be answered in different ways.
- Observe closely using simple equipment.
- Perform simple tests.
- Identify and classify.
- Use observations and ideas to suggest answers to questions.
- Gather and record data to help in answering questions.

Lower Key Stage 2 (Years 3 and 4)

- Ask relevant questions and use different types of scientific enquiries to answer them.
- Set up simple practical enquiries, comparative and fair tests.
- Make systematic and careful observations and, where appropriate, take accurate measurements using standard units, using a range of equipment including thermometers and data loggers.
- Gather, record, classify and present data in a variety of ways to help in answering questions.
- Record findings using simple scientific language, drawings, labelled diagrams, keys, bar charts and tables.
- Report on findings from enquiries, including oral and written explanations, displays or presentations of results and conclusions.
- Use results to draw simple conclusions, make predictions for new values, suggest improvements and raise further questions.
- Identify differences, similarities or changes related to simple scientific ideas and processes.
- Use straightforward scientific evidence to answer questions or to support their findings.

Upper Key Stage 2 (Years 5 and 6)

- Plan different types of scientific enquiries to answer questions, including recognising and controlling variables, where necessary.
- Take measurements using a range of scientific equipment, with increasing accuracy and precision, taking repeat readings when appropriate.
- Record data and results of increasing complexity using scientific diagrams and labels, classification keys, tables, scatter graphs, bar and line graphs.
- Use test results to make predictions to set up further comparative and fair tests.
- Report and present findings from enquiries, including conclusions, causal relationships and explanations of and degree of trust in results, in oral and written forms such as displays and other presentations.
- Identify scientific evidence that has been used to support or refute ideas or arguments.

Figure 1.1 Working scientifically (taken from the National Curriculum in England: Science programmes of study, 2015).

Why bother teaching 'Working scientifically'?

Apart from the obvious answer that it is fun and a part of a broad and balanced curriculum, first and foremost:

It can have a massive impact on progress, attainment and engagement in Science. As Ofsted note in their 'Successful Science' report (2011: 6):

> In the schools which showed clear improvement in science subjects, key factors in promoting students' engagement, learning and progress were more practical science lessons and the development of the skills of scientific enquiry.

It allows us to find out what the children's ideas are. Quite simply, children's ideas are important. Children's ideas develop from interaction with their environment (I take environment to mean the physical world and the sum total of interactions in a child's life). Much research has been done on this – you may have come across Piaget, Vygotsky, Bruner, Osborne and Freyberg in your studies. As Harlen and Qualter (2015) emphasise, we must use children's ideas as the starting point in developing scientific ideas. However, children's ideas that start in early childhood, borne out of experience of the world around them and how they interact with that world, are often in conflict with the scientific ideas contained in a formalised curriculum. These 'alternative' ideas or as some name them, 'misconceptions', can represent a huge barrier to progress, and unless they are thoroughly explored we cannot possibly hope to overcome them. Working scientifically allows us to see these 'misconceptions' and gives us the opportunity to correct them.

It is crucial to facilitate progress in conceptual understanding. The process skills contained in working scientifically and the scientific attitudes it develops are key to helping children make progress. Through exploration and investigation children can ask questions to test their ideas and seek answers to the questions they ask. For example, a child may be utterly convinced that all heavy objects sink. It is only when the child explores a number of objects and sees that some heavy objects do indeed float that this persistent idea can be explored and challenged and they can move past this to a greater understanding of the concepts contained in this (deceptively simple) phenomenon. The ideas that do not fit the evidence from the enquiry process usually are rejected and sometimes a fundamental shift or 'penny drop moment' can be achieved.

It helps maintain positive scientific attitudes. As reported in Ofsted's 'Maintaining Curiosity' report (2013), scientific enquiry is crucial to developing and sustaining curiosity, and this, in turn, is an important factor in the development of the young scientist. Sadly, as the curriculum becomes more formal and content-driven, children lose some of the wonder, curiosity and excitement that science promotes. Keeping enquiry alive is crucial in maintaining these positive attitudes and will, in the long run, help you in your teaching. It can well promote science as a future career for children.

It models how scientists work. Working scientifically allows us to develop an understanding within children of how scientists work in the real world. The myth of the ever-wise male with a white coat, frizzy hair and goggles can be challenged and children can learn that *anyone* can be a scientist. As Driver et al. (1996) note, children have a fairly limited view of how science works and the nature of science; only when they are older do they develop the idea of testing ideas and seeking evidence. We can develop this idea a lot earlier by modelling the scientific method and developing an appreciation of the tenuous nature of scientific ideas and evidence. The initial stages of stimulating a child's imagination and natural curiosity can lead to questions being asked and predictions and tentative hypotheses made. From there we can then encourage children to explore the range of ways of finding out answers to then testing their ideas, making observations and presenting what they find out. We can encourage reflection on the original

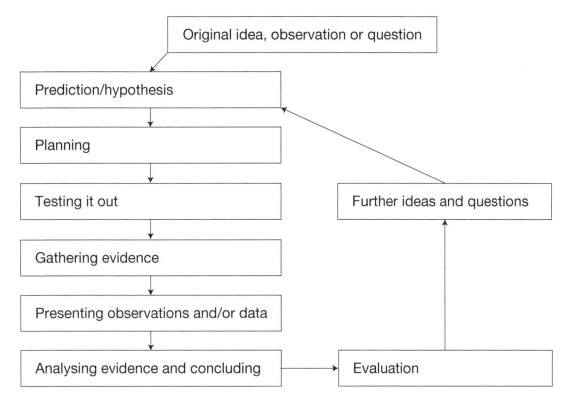

Figure 1.2 The scientific method.

question and make tentative conclusions that might need further testing, which can lead to a whole new prediction and investigation.

From this process we can encourage a period of reflection and evaluation to see if what they have done was fit for purpose and actually could answer the question. This process is one that is performed every day by scientists in the real world and by providing exposure to this process we model the way that scientists work scientifically. This, in turn, can help throw light on an area that is full of misconceptions and stereotypes and thus promote positive scientific attitudes. We can only do this if we 'work scientifically'.

How do we teach 'Working scientifically'?

A rather glib answer to this question is 'just do a practical activity' and I cannot dispute the value of a well-placed practical activity. However, does this actually teach the skills? I do not think so. To teach the skills is an active process and requires an organised approach. This might be taken as me devaluing open-ended, child-led exploration, but this is not the case.

In the early stages of learning a skill, initial experience *is* vital. This comes from an early age (in the Early Years and Foundation Stage) through exploration of the world around them. Much of this is done unconsciously and one of the key features of learning the skills at this stage is observation. This requires different, less formal pedagogy and is centred on *play and exploration*. As we move through the years, the curriculum becomes more formalised and the skills more structured and demanding, and this will affect the approaches a teacher takes, the contexts they use and the experiences the children have. As a result, investigations usually lose the element of 'play' and might take on a more serious tone.

An example would be children playing with objects in the paddling pool. What transforms this from being simple play to development of a skill is the teacher. A skilled teacher can use this as an opportunity to ask questions of the children, encourage them to observe what is going on and to make some tentative predictions. Later in primary science a fish tank might replace the paddling pool and a more formal exploration of which objects float and which objects sink might take place; even more formal would be to supply the children with a hypothesis such as 'all heavy objects sink' for them to investigate.

'Working scientifically' skills are usually taught through a range of enquiries (questions to be answered) and investigations (ways to answer the question). They are best located in a context, either something imaginative like a character in a book answering a question, or with a specific section of the programme of study related to knowledge and understanding. There are a range of investigations that children can participate in to develop their skills and their conceptual understanding. These are:

- observing over time
- pattern seeking
- identifying, classifying and grouping
- comparative and fair testing (controlled investigations)
- researching using secondary sources.

National Curriculum in England: Science programme of study, 2015: 31–32

Although there are a range of investigations that can be used, the AKSIS Project (ASE – King's College London Science Investigations in Schools 1998, and subsequent publications from Goldsworthy et al.) indicated a very limited set of investigations in use at Key Stages 2 and 3 and the dominant type of investigation being a fair test (50.4 per cent).

The issue with this, as Harlen and Qualter (2015) note, is that it is 'rarely feasible' for children to cover the whole range of activities and skills in any one enquiry, thus the dominance of the 'fair test' investigation represents a huge missed opportunity to develop the rest of the skills and for children to truly progress their understanding.

So, can we *teach individual skills in isolation*? For example, drawing a graph. This is certainly a valid approach for a discrete skill and there are plenty of publications that deal explicitly with this, such as Goldsworthy et al.'s *Getting to Grips with Graphs* (2000). But if doing this they really should be located in a context of the theme or the topic taught. You will notice in this guide I have illustrated this approach by providing different contexts to explore the skills.

What about *techniques and resources*? There is an incredible range of techniques and resources out there. You only need to scan the TES resources page to see them. I do not advocate the use of any particular technique or resource as any activity must be adapted to the needs of the children you are teaching. I do, however, firmly believe that whatever technique or resource you choose to use, a key feature must be dialogue and questioning between child and peers and child and teacher. This is essential for development of the skill because in the initial stages effective questioning and dialogue can reveal the level of understanding and make apparent misconceptions and misunderstandings about the skill, for example in technical language or the language of measurement. It can also make conscious thought more conscious and therefore bring about a new way of thinking about the skills. Therefore, a key feature of this guide is the suggestion of activities where the teacher eavesdrops, encourages talk, asks questions and models the processes and language required to be successful in the skill.

Another important feature of teaching 'Working scientifically' is to *support literacy*. It is important for the expression of what the children think, how they will investigate, and presentation of what they have found out and what it all means. The ability to effectively communicate in science can be challenging because we have our own set of subject-specific vocabulary that we expect the children to be able to access and use. We also have specific types of writing for

---

Exploring and deconstructing a sample text.

Establishing the ground rules for writing the text.

Sharing ideas and constructing together an example of the text.

Independently writing the text.

Figure 1.3 A basic sequence for teaching specific writing.

specific purposes, for example the method, the conclusion or analysis, and the evaluation. I have seen many children engage in investigative work yet get frustrated as they cannot express what they have found out in the form that the teacher wants.

For this reason, I have included two specific strategies that work. The first is a set of scaffold mats, each named after the skill. The purpose of these mats is to provide the vocabulary and sentence structures that children might need to express themselves in the skill area. The second technique involves an adaptation of a sequence for teaching writing (see Figure 1.3) developed in the National Literacy Strategy (1998–2010) and by the Science strand of the secondary National Strategy in the 'Literacy in Science' (2002) professional development units. This technique gets children to think about the formal structure of the writing that they are required to complete. I have included suggestions of how this might be run as an intervention in Years 5 and 6.

Progress in 'Working scientifically'

Progress for children is far more useful to discuss than attainment. It is complex and is influenced by any number of variables (such as starting point, language, cognitive development etc.). Just as in conceptual understanding, progress in working scientifically doesn't 'just happen'. To do this we must understand the starting point for the child and then what is the next 'step' for a child. Previously, progress in the skills that 'Working scientifically' encompassed was measured in levels by (in part) the SATs tests and teacher assessment. *'Assessing Pupil Progress' (APP)* in science (2009) (see Figure 1.4) was an example of the attempt to tease apart progress in the skills and went a great way in helping teachers. However, it was found to be onerous and bureaucratic by many who attempted it (although it was a very valid and important piece of work with many strengths).

The new National Curriculum in England: Science programmes of study no longer measures progress in levels but provides us with a set of age-related expectations, or ARE (for example, see Figure 1.5) and national standards. These show us what the pupils should be able to do at the end of the key milestones contained in the curriculum: Years 1 and 2, Years 3 and 4, and Years 5 and 6. (Note that although knowledge and understanding is further divided into individual years, 'Working scientifically' is banded into two years.) The model of progress I will use in this guide is based around these ARE, will use the language of the National Curriculum, and divide those skills into 'basic' and 'advanced'. It will also use the non-statutory notes and guidance to further exemplify these.

Level 1

Across a range of contexts and practical situations pupils:

- respond to prompts by making some simple suggestions about how to find an answer or make observations
- use their senses and simple equipment to make observations.

Level 2

Across a range of contexts and practical situations pupils:

- make some suggestions about how to find things out or how to collect data to answer a question or idea they are investigating
- identify things to measure or observe that are relevant to the question or idea they are investigating
- correctly use equipment provided to make observations and measurements
- make measurements, using standard or non-standard units as appropriate.

Figure 1.4 An example of progression from primary science APP (2009).

Lower primary **Years 1 and 2**	Ask simple questions and recognise they can be answered in different ways.
Lower Key Stage 2 **Years 3 and 4**	Ask relevant questions and use different types of scientific enquiries to answer them.
Upper Key Stage 2 **Years 5 and 6**	Plan different types of scientific enquiries to answer questions, including recognising and controlling variables, where necessary. Use test results to make predictions to set up further comparative and fair tests.

Figure 1.5 Progress in ARE in the skill area of raising questions, predicting and planning (National Curriculum in England: Science programmes of study, 2015).

What is contained in this guide?

This guide is not a scheme of work, but it gives you the opportunities to develop and practise the working scientifically skills in context. Each chapter focuses on a skill. Contained therein is:

- a brief summary of the theory behind the skill
- a brief summary of the major steps in progress for each skill
- an indication of relevant mathematical skills that might be needed to develop the skill
- a discussion of some of the barriers to learning for each skill
- a brief teaching sequence to explore and develop the skill
- a list of key questions you can ask when you are working with the children to get them to think about the skill
- a set of self-assessment sheets for children to use
- a set of generic assessment sheets for the teacher
- planning mats to support the learning and development of the language required at two different levels: basic and more advanced.

Within this guide, if your children are Years 1 and 2 they will be expected to operate at Year 1 and 2 expectations. The first activity will allow you to explore, develop and consolidate that ARE in context. There will also be an activity to move them to exceeding ARE.

If your children are Years 3 and 4 they will be expected to operate at Year 3 and 4 ARE. If they are not, then there will be an activity in context to consolidate Year 1 and 2 ARE and then provide the bridge to Years 3 and 4 ARE. If they are working at the ARE there will also be an activity to move them to exceeding ARE.

If your children are Years 5 and 6 they will be expected to operate at Year 5 and 6 ARE. If they are not, then there will be an activity in context to consolidate Year 3 and 4 ARE and then provide the bridge to Year 5 and 6 ARE.

You will be given multiple contexts to explore the skills. You will notice that I have used fairly common questions that can be used as whole investigations if you wish. My purpose is to illustrate how, with some minor tweaking, you can use these investigations to teach individual skills. You can also use these activities as means to develop knowledge and understanding or after a teaching sequence of knowledge and understanding. It is your choice.

They are as follows:

Skill area	Years 1 + 2	Years 3 + 4	Years 5 + 6
Raising questions/ predicting/planning	Investigating the weather	Investigating shadow puppets	Investigating gears, levers and pulleys
Observation, measuring and recording	Investigating plants	Investigating sound	Investigating fossils
Analysing/conclusions	Investigating seeds and bulbs	Investigating rocks and soil	Investigating circulation
Evaluating investigations	Investigating habitats	Investigating teeth	Investigating materials

2 Raising questions, predictions and planning

Raising questions, predicting and planning is a cluster of skills usually found at the beginning of the process of investigating, often thought of as just 'planning', but each skill needs to be thought about carefully and explicitly taught. Usually the whole process begins with an experience, observation or a question that needs to be explored and investigated, which can then be developed into a relevant enquiry with a more formalised structure involving different investigative approaches.

Figure 2.1 shows the skills progression in the National Curriculum in England: Science programmes of study. Progress within these group of skills starts with the skill to ask a question, come up with some ideas of how to get an answer and to explore different ways to answer the question. Here it is important that children are provided with the stimulus to ask different questions and then experience the range of explorations suggested. It is important at this stage to realise that a full-blown fair test investigation is *not* appropriate and that the types of investigation tend to be more observational. With more experience of the range of explorations, the next step is that the children should be able to refine their understanding of different types of questions and ways of answering questions, rephrasing questions into forms that can be explored and that can be answered using an investigation. Here the children should work towards selecting the best approach. The final step in progress is much bigger as it introduces the notion of variables and comparative and fair testing (controlled investigations). There is a consequence here for the teacher to introduce a more formalised approach towards planning and the skills that the children need to develop to be successful in this set of ARE.

Looking at this in another way and in a bit more detail, we can gain a sense of what skills might be inherent in these steps yet not explicitly mentioned – those that are earlier in the development and later in the development. This, in turn, gives us an idea of what we need to plan and to assess to facilitate development. Examples of this are skills in predicting and identifying variables.

To plan effectively we not only need to be aware of the steps in progress, but of those factors that can be considered to be barriers to progress and therefore would need to be considered when planning a teaching sequence or lessons. Although the list below is not exhaustive it will raise your awareness of these.

Lower primary Years 1 and 2	**Ask simple questions and recognise they can be answered in different ways** *Guidance (non-statutory)* Pupils in Years 1 and 2 should explore the world around them and raise their own questions. They should experience different types of scientific enquiries, including practical activities, and begin to recognise ways in which they might answer scientific questions.
Lower Key Stage 2 Years 3 and 4	**Ask relevant questions and use different types of scientific enquiries to answer them** *Guidance (non-statutory)* Pupils in Years 3 and 4 should be given a range of scientific experiences to enable them to raise their own questions about the world around them. They should start to make their own decisions about the most appropriate type of scientific enquiry they might use to answer questions; recognise when a simple fair test is necessary and help to decide how to set it up.
Upper Key Stage 2 Years 5 and 6	**Plan different types of scientific enquiries to answer questions, including recognising and controlling variables, where necessary** **Using test results to make predictions to set up further comparative and fair tests** *Guidance (non-statutory)* Pupils in Years 5 and 6 should use their science experiences to: explore ideas and raise different kinds of questions; select and plan the most appropriate type of scientific enquiry to use to answer scientific questions; recognise when and how to set up comparative and fair tests and explain which variables need to be controlled and why.

Figure 2.1 Progress in ARE in the skill area of raising questions, predicting and planning (National Curriculum in England: Science programmes of study, 2015).

Basic skills	Advanced skills
Asking simple questions	Refining questions into a form that can be investigated
Exploring different ways to answer a question	Identifying the way in which to best answer the question using a specific investigation
Exploring what has changed/what they could change	Identifying and naming variables
Making simple predictions, usually in the form of answering their question	Consciously making predictions related to the variables in the enquiry using precise language related to causality
Little independence in decision-making and being given instructions by the teacher	More independence in decision-making to making own choices on types of equipment and how to use it, observations to make and frequency
Showing you what they are doing but cannot explain why they are doing it	Plan in advance what they will do and explain to you why
Using familiar contexts and examples	Investigating less familiar examples and contexts

Figure 2.2 Key steps in progress for raising questions and planning.

Barriers to progress

Adults limiting the question. Here the teacher could, with the best intentions, supply the pupils with a question that needs to be explored. This is certainly valid and can be used, but this takes away the first step in development – the ability to be curious and ask questions. This is particularly important in the earlier years when questions are often spontaneous and born out of play and exploration, but can be equally important in more formal investigations. For example, there is a big difference in the experience for the child if they are given the question 'What can affect heart rate?' compared to 'How can exercise affect heart rate?' The latter narrows down the variables to be looked at whereas the former can lead to all kinds of rich questions and predictions. If you are to supply a question ensure the skill you are developing is not the ability to ask questions but to plan to answer the question.

Adults limiting the investigation. As already noted in the introduction, some teachers limit investigations to 'fair test' only. The important point to note is that planning is not just limited to fair tests. Other types of investigation all need to be planned for as well. For example, in observation-based enquiries the children will need to plan what to observe, how to observe and what they will use to make those observations.

Confusion with the language of variables. This is a common area with children (and sometimes teachers). Although variables are explicitly mentioned in the ARE for Years 5 and 6 there is no clear time when it is appropriate to introduce the concept of the variable or to change the language used to express variables – for example, moving from the word 'factor' to the word 'variable'. If it is implicit in the ARE for Years 3 and 4 to introduce the fair test investigation as a viable way of exploring different types of investigation should we then introduce the word 'variable'? You need to judge this carefully as introduction too early can be a barrier to learning. Whatever language you judge to be most appropriate must be used consistently.

Misconceptions with variables. Most children's alternative conceptions come from everyday experience, so if we talk about the two variables in a simple causal relationship (input and output) then it is tempting to think nothing else can have an effect on the outcome. Hence we arrive at the idea of a 'fair test'. Some children believe that the only variable you need to control is the one you are exploring. This ultimately leads to an 'unfair test'. While this might be acceptable when you are working at ARE Years 3 and 4 by ARE Years 5 and 6 we would expect children to move beyond this.

Independence. It is sometimes tempting to intervene when a pupil is struggling to make decisions. Care is needed as independence in decision-making is a key step in progress for this area at ARE Years 3 and 4 and by ARE Years 5 and 6 should be well established.

Resources. Not having a wide variety of resources for the children to explore and imagine using can often limit what they can identify 'planning' with. You can almost bet that if children's imagination is given free rein they will come up with all kinds of wonderful ideas that you might not have anticipated. If you do not have resources available, ensure the children can ask you what it is possible to get for them to use and allow time for preparation.

General suggestions for the teacher

Developing the skill of raising questions and questioning

1 Encourage play and exploration of familiar objects or experiences. Then move to less familiar objects etc.
2 Develop a climate for learning that encourages and nurtures curiosity. Invite questions by having a question wall/board with callouts associated with a theme, event or object and develop a climate for learning where it is safe to get things wrong.
3 Develop your own bank of questions that encourage and facilitate question asking such as 'What would you like to know?', 'What is that?', 'If it could answer you, what would you ask it?'
4 Help children refine their questions into a more investigable form by helping them focus on an outcome. Much of this will depend on the type of enquiry the question relates to. For example, what do you need to find out?
5 Have the question stems (sentence starters of 'what' 'where' etc.) displayed on paddles so that children can hold up a paddle to ask a question.
6 Play 'Who/what am I?' by sticking a word on a child's forehead and inviting them to ask questions to guess what they are.
7 Give children a stimulus and ask them to create a set number of questions in a set time.
8 Get children to work in groups to generate their own questions.
9 Use KWL grids (what I know, what I would like to find out, and what I have learnt) as a way into developing the children's own questions.
10 Use question grids with question stems and connectives to help frame questions. (You might see these referred to as 'Q charts'.)
11 Allow time for the children to talk and develop a fixed number of questions or as many as they can think of in a fixed period of time.
12 Develop a key vocabulary bank to assist in the formulation of questions and display it.

Developing the skill of planning and controlling variables

1 Develop an early understanding of the different types of enquiry through direct experience. Gradually encourage the children to match the experience to a question.

2 Provide opportunities for planning by starting with a question to be answered by exploration without giving instructions. Use the questions, 'How might you do this?', 'What do you need to find out?', 'What do you need to do to find out?'

3 Scaffold initial attempts at planning a fair test by using the planning mat in the resources section of this guide.

4 Develop the idea of a range of variables within contexts related to content and consider having a separate teaching sequence for this skill. This approach can be found and explored further in the CASE project (Cognitive Acceleration in Science Education, King's College London) and 'Let's think science' materials (at letsthink.org.uk).

5 Explore the idea of variables you can change and how they affect outcomes in a range of practical situations.

6 Provide a number of different independent variables with values and match the variable to the value.

7 Talk through different inquiries that have been planned and/or completed to identify how they could have been improved.

8 Provide opportunities to look at investigations where the variables have been controlled and have not been controlled and the subsequent outcomes, and check if they are relevant.

9 To encourage reflection on planning, always ask 'Would this answer the question?'

10 Model a deliberately unfair investigation and ask the children to correct you! Or ask 'How will you make it fair?'

Questions to help develop raising questions, predictions and planning

What would you like to know?
What is your question?
What do you need to find out?
Can you tell me something you know about that?
What would you like to do?
What do you think the answer will be?
How could you answer that question?
Will that answer your question?
What kind of investigation do you want to use?
Can you think of another way of doing that?
What do you think will happen?
Why do you think this will happen?
What equipment do you want to use?
Why do you want to use that piece of equipment?
How is 'x' different to 'y'?
How do you think that will change?
What could you change?
What will you keep the same?
Which variable could you keep the same?
How do we make it fair?

Would that be fair?
How could you change…?
Is that fair?
What will that measure?
What will you measure?
How will you measure that?
How often do you need to measure that?
Can you think of a better way of measuring that?
Can you think of a better piece of equipment to use?

There follows three contexts to explore and develop the skill of raising questions, predicting and planning, which directly relate to the new programme of study. These are:

Years 1 and 2 – Investigating the weather
Years 3 and 4 – Investigating shadows
Years 5 and 6 – Investigating gears, pulleys and levers.

Raising questions, predictions and planning

Years 1 and 2: Investigating the weather

Working scientifically

Working at age-related expectations

Ask simple questions and recognise they can be answered in different ways.

Working above age-related expectations

Ask relevant questions and use different types of scientific enquiries to answer them.

Knowledge and understanding

Working at age-related expectations

Observe changes across the four seasons.

Observe and describe weather associated with the seasons and how day length varies.

Mathematics

Working at age-related expectations

Number
Count to and across 100, forwards and backwards, beginning with 0 or 1, or from any given number.

Count, read and write numbers to 100 in numerals; count in multiples of twos, fives and tens.

Given a number, identify one more and one less.

Identify and represent numbers using objects and pictorial representations including the number line, and use the language of: equal to, more than, less than (fewer), most, least.

Read and write numbers from 1 to 20 in numerals and words.

Measurement
Measure and begin to record the following: lengths and heights.

Compare, describe and solve practical problems for: lengths and heights (for example, long/short, longer/shorter, tall/short, double/half).

Teacher information

Weather can be thought of as the conditions in the atmosphere over a short period of time, for example during the course of a day. Climate can be thought of as the weather conditions of a region, such as temperature, air pressure, humidity, precipitation (rainfall), sunshine, cloudiness and winds over a longer period of time. This can vary from place to place due to interaction between all these factors within the area.

The common language for weather we use at this level is: sunny, cloudy, rainy, snow, hot, cold, windy, wet, dry.

The children at this stage will need to experience how weather can change across a period of time to give us seasonal variations.

The weather is also linked to daylight hours and this can be explored with children over a period of time – for example, the number of daylight hours in winter compared to summer.

Launch pad

Give out the launch pad activity and introduce the context for exploring the weather. Use a suitable story or poem to introduce the context of the weather. Look at the weather today and ask the children what they would like to know about the weather.

Encourage the children to formulate a question or two about the weather. Get them to record their questions around the stimulus pictures or on a large piece of paper or record which student asks which question.

Now pose the question, 'How could you find that out?' Record their responses and allow them to try out their ideas. Remember this is your base-line assessment so do not intervene at this point. If they are struggling to suggest ways to find out, they can put 'I do not know' or a '?'.

Ask the children to complete the first column of the self-assessment sheet.

Activity 1

Target group: Years 1 and 2 who are working at ARE.
Aim: To develop simple questions.

What to do

Provide a variety of stimuli about the weather at the time of year you are carrying out this sequence. Encourage talk for a while about the weather today and invite children to draw or write their responses (some might use oral explanations) and display responses on a learning wall. Now think about the rain on a rainy day. Encourage questions about the rain. Use the basic planning mat (see Appendix) to help formulate the questions. Model one question formulation about the weather: 'How much rain falls over a week?'

The final part is to provide stimulus for different ways to answer the question. Have around the room the means to answer 'generally' the questions. Elicit ideas on how they might find out some answers. Now as a class discuss how many ways they have come up with to answer their question and collate the responses on a learning wall. Now explain the best way to answer this question is that you need to collect rain water to measure how much has fallen.

Choose with the children the containers they want to use and carry out the exploration. After a suitable period of time, explore with the children which container collected the most rain water.

Tips

- Allow sufficient time for exploration and play.
- Go outside and look at the weather over a number of days to stimulate talk and questions.
- Develop a key vocabulary bank to assist in the formulation of questions.
- Have the question stems laminated so that if a child wants to ask a question they can pick up the question stem and hold it up and orally ask their question.
- Ask the children to take their question on a sticky note to a piece of equipment/area in the classroom that refers to their question.

Key questions to develop the skill

- What are you looking at/playing with/reading? What do you like about it?
- What does it do?
- I wonder…? Do you think…?
- What would you like to know more about?
- What do you want to find out?
- How could you do that? What do you need to do? What about if we did this…?

Key vocabulary

Question stems: what, when, why, where, how

Questions, investigate, ideas

Resources

A book corner filled with books on weather, a computer open with information about the weather, observing equipment, craft equipment, etc.

To make a simple weather station go to:

http://www.metofficeexampleov.uk/education/kids/things-to-do/weather-station

Activity 2

Target group: Years 1 and 2 who are working above ARE.
Aim: To develop approaches to answering questions.

What to do

Ask children to look at the weather today. Use the basic planning mat (see Appendix) to help formulate the questions. Model one question formulation about the weather and then highlight the main planning stems and connectives in the body of the question. Allow children to brainstorm for a while their own questions using the planning mat and display responses on a learning wall. Using the basic planning mat, ask them to develop two specific questions about the weather to answer requiring different investigative methods. Collate all the answers around the learning wall. Ask them also to come up with a way to answer their questions and record these methods on the learning wall also. Come up with a list of 'scientific ways to answer a question' – cross-reference with the basic planning mat.

Now provide the children with a range of questions about the weather, such as:

- How much rain falls in a week? (observation over time)
- How does the temperature change in London across a whole year? (pattern seeking)
- Where are the hottest countries? (research, identification and classification)
- How windy is it today? (observation)
- What is the weather like in Athens today? (research)
- Does most rain fall in spring or autumn? (research and pattern seeking)
- Where in the UK does most snow fall? (research and pattern seeking)
- How much rain fell today? (observation over time)
- Which countries are the driest? (research and classification)
- Which countries are the hottest and which are the coldest? (research and classification)
- Are windier days colder? (basic fair test investigation, observation over time)

Have around the room different ways to answer these questions. Group the children and give them a specific question. Look at the options of how to answer the questions. Ask the children to match the question with the method that was used while at the same time exploring the ways to answer it. Then provide the rest of the questions related to the weather and ask them to match the question with the method.

Tips

- Ensure the children understand that multiple methods can be used to answer some questions.
- Ask the children to rank the ways of finding out the answers and then make a judgement on the best way to answer the question.
- Carry this out as a group activity, encouraging talk in the investigations.

Key questions to develop the skill

- What could you do to find out this answer? Could you do something else?
- Could you think of another way to answer the question? Which way do you think is best?

Key vocabulary

Question, investigation, ideas, answers, spring, autumn, winter, summer, rain, sun, snow, wind, temperature, hot, cold

Resources

A book corner filled with books on weather, a computer open with information about the weather, observing equipment, craft equipment, etc.

To make a simple weather station go to:

http://www.metofficexampleov.uk/education/kids/things-to-do/weather-station

The final activity

Repeat the launch pad activity.

Give out the self-assessment sheet and ask children to complete the second column.

Raising questions, predictions and planning

Years 3 and 4: Investigating shadows

Working scientifically

Working towards age-related expectations

Ask simple questions and recognise they can be answered in different ways.

Working at age-related expectations

Ask relevant questions and use different types of scientific enquiries to answer them.

Working above age-related expectations

Plan different types of scientific enquiries to answer questions, including recognising and controlling variables, where necessary.

Using test results to make predictions to set up further comparative and fair tests.

Knowledge and understanding

Working at age-related expectations

Recognise that shadows are formed when the light from a light source is blocked by a solid object.

Find patterns in the way that the size of shadows change.

Mathematics

Working at age-related expectations (Year 3)

Number
Count from 0 in multiples of 4, 8, 50 and 100.

Find 10 or 100 more or less than a given number.

Recognise the place value of each digit in a three-digit number (hundreds, tens, ones).

Compare and order numbers up to 1000.

Identify, represent and estimate numbers using different representations.

Read and write numbers up to 1000 in numerals and in words.

Measurement
Measure, compare, add and subtract: lengths (m/cm/mm); mass (kg/g); volume/capacity (l/ml).

Measure the perimeter of simple 2D shapes.

Teacher information

Light is needed in order to see things and dark is the absence of light. If light passes through a material it is known as transparent; if it only partially passes through the material it is known as translucent. If light cannot pass through a material the material is known as opaque.

When light is blocked by an opaque material or a solid object a shadow is formed. This shadow will resemble the object, but will change in appearance and size depending on the distance between the screen the shadow appears on and the object or the distance between the light source and the object.

- If an object is moved **closer** (distance decreased) to the light source, the shadow gets bigger.
- If an object is moved **further** (distance increased) away from the light source, the shadow gets smaller.
- If a screen is moved closer to the object (distance decreases) the shadow gets larger.
- If a screen is moved further away from the object (distance increases) the shadow gets smaller.

Variables or factors are the things you can change, control or measure. The key is consistent use of language, for example 'How does the size of the puppet affect the size of the shadow?' For your reference the language of variables is displayed below.

The size of the puppet = input variable = the variable we can change = the independent variable.

The size of the shadow = output variable = the variable we measure = the results = the dependent variable.

Launch pad

Give out the launch pad activity. Introduce the context that the children are exploring shadows. Show a relevant example. Encourage the children to formulate a question or two about the shadows. Get them to record their questions around the central stimulus picture.

Now ask them how they will find out the answer to each question. Get them to record their answers on their paper.

Remember this is your base-line assessment so do not intervene at this point. If they are struggling to suggest ways to find out, they can put 'I do not know' or a '?'.

Ask the children to complete the first column of the self-assessment sheet.

Activity 1

Target group: Years 3 and 4 who are working towards ARE.
Aim: To develop simple questions.

What to do

Prompted by a shadow puppet explain that we want to find out how it works and how to make the clearest and biggest shadows from them.

Use the basic planning mat (see Appendix) to help formulate the questions. Model one question formulation about the puppet and then highlight the main question stems and connectives in the main body of the question. Allow children to brainstorm their own questions for a while using the planning mat and display responses on a learning wall. The final part involves providing stimulus to explore different ways to answer the question. Have around the room the means and equipment to answer 'generally' the questions. Elicit ideas on how the children might find out some answers. Now as a class discuss how many ways they have come up with to answer their question and collate the responses on a learning wall.

Allow the children to choose one question and try to answer it with their selected method. Move around the room posing questions about their planning.

Key questions to develop the skill

- What would you like to find out about?
- What kinds of questions could you ask?
- Can you think of another way to ask that question?
- Are there any questions we cannot answer?
- Can you see in the room something you could use to help you answer the question?
- How will that help you answer the question?
- Is that the best way to answer the question?

Key vocabulary

Question stems: what, when, why, where, how

Questions, investigate, ideas

Resources

Light sources, for example torches or direction lamps

Shadow puppets or the means to make shadow puppets

Rulers

Graph paper

Activity 2

Target group: Years 3 and 4 who are working at ARE.
Aim: To develop approaches to answer questions.

What to do

Ask the children to look at a shadow puppet. Use the basic planning mat (see Appendix) to help formulate the questions. Model one question formulation about the puppet and then highlight the main question stems and connectives in the main body of the question. Allow children to brainstorm their own questions for a while using the planning mat and display responses on a learning wall. Using the basic question mat, ask them to develop two specific questions about the puppet to answer requiring different investigative methods. Collate all the answers around the learning wall. Ask them also to come up with a way to answer their questions and record these methods on the learning wall. Come up with a list of scientific ways to answer a question – cross-reference with the basic planning mat.

Now provide the children with a range of questions about shadow puppets, such as:

- How do I make a shadow from the puppet? (observation)
- What is the best material to make a shadow puppet from? (research, classification)
- Why do shadows look the same as the puppet? (observation, research)
- What light source makes the best shadows? (observation)
- Why do shadows look bigger if I move the puppet away from the light source? (research, observation)
- What happens to the shadow as I change the distance between the puppet and light source? (observation)
- Does the distance between the puppet and light source change the size of the shadow? (fair test)
- Which countries use puppets to tell stories? (research)
- What is the best material to make a shadow puppet from? (research, observation, classification)
- How does distance affect the size of the shadow? (fair test)
- What have shadow puppets traditionally been made of? (research)
- Does the size of the puppet matter? (fair test)
- Can translucent materials make good shadow puppets? (research, observation, classification)

Have around the room different ways to answer these questions. Group the children and give them a specific question and look at the options of how to answer the questions. Ask the children to match the question with the method that was used while at the same time exploring the ways to answer it. Then provide the rest of the questions related to shadow puppets and ask them to match the question with the method.

Tips

- Ensure there are some questions that have multiple methods to answer them.
- Ask the children to rank the ways of finding out the answers and then make a judgement on the best way to answer the question.
- Carry this out as a group activity, encouraging talk in the investigations.

Key questions to develop the skill

- What could you do to find out this answer? Could you do something else?
- Could you think of another way to answer the question? Which way do you think is best?

Key vocabulary

Question, investigation, ideas, answers, distance, opaque, light source, shadow, size, material, transparent

Resources

Different light sources, both in size and intensity of light bulbs

Different materials such as card, paper, cardboard, plastic acetate sheet

Rulers (different sizes)

Basic planning mat

Activity 3

Target group: Years 3 and 4 who are working above ARE.
Aim: To develop the skill of planning investigations.

What to do

Provide children with a specific question to answer relating to the shadow puppet context requiring comparative and fair testing (see the list in Activity 2). Use the advanced planning mats to model and explore with them the variables and what they think might happen. Ask them to follow the investigation to see if they have answered the question (the focus should not be on the write-up or presentation of results as we are interested in structure of the planning).

Now provide the children with three methods based on answering the one question. Ask them to discuss the methods and agree on which one is the best. Now using the children's input come up with a list of rules for planning a fair test investigation. Refer to the advanced planning mat to model how we identify variables. Take another question and draft a method together with the children, using the rules.

Use the advanced planning mat to formulate sentences, explaining at each point why we use this language.

Tips

- The concept of the fair test is tricky. It might require a separate teaching sequence.
- Don't get hung up on the language of variables – it is enough to refer to them as 'factors' or even 'things', just be consistent.
- For a more kinaesthetic, whole-class way to model planning, use the planning posters developed by the National Strategies (see Bibliography).
- Always refer their plan back to the original question. With controlled investigations the clue to the variables is located in the question.
- Carry this out as a group activity, encouraging talk in the investigations.

Key questions to develop the skill

- What could you do to find out this answer? Could you do something else?
- Could you think of another way to answer the question? Which way do you think is best?
- What could you change in this investigation? What will you keep the same to make it fair?
- What will you measure in this investigation?
- What do you think will happen based on what you have found out so far?
- Can you think of another question to ask and what will happen?

Key vocabulary

Question, investigation, ideas, answers, distance, opaque, light source, shadow, size, material, transparent

Resources

Light sources, for example torches

Material to make shadow puppets

Shadow puppet templates (if required)

Rulers (different sizes)

Wall or card to act as a screen

Blackout room

Advanced planning mat

The final activity

Explore again the children's launch pad activity/poster of questions about shadow puppets and ways to answer them. Ask them to annotate and amend it, add some more questions and suggest a way of answering them.

Give out the final self-assessment sheet and ask children to complete the second column.

Raising questions, predictions and planning

Years 5 and 6: Investigating gears, pulleys and levers

Working scientifically

Working towards age-related expectations

Ask relevant questions and use different types of scientific enquiries to answer them.

Working at age-related expectations

Plan different types of scientific enquiries to answer questions, including recognising and controlling variables, where necessary.

Using test results to make predictions to set up further comparative and fair tests.

Knowledge and understanding

Working at age-related expectations (Year 5)

Recognise that some mechanisms, including levers, pulleys and gears, allow a smaller force to have a greater effect.

Non-statutory guidance: Pupils should explore the effects of levers, pulleys and simple machines on movement.

They might design and make products that use levers, pulleys, gears and/or springs and explore their effects.

Mathematics

Working at age-related expectations (Year 5)

Number
Read, write, order and compare numbers to at least 1,000,000 and determine the value of each digit.

Count forwards or backwards in steps of powers of 10 for any given number up to 1,000,000.

Measurement
Convert between different units of metric measure (for example, kilometre and metre; centimetre and metre; centimetre and millimetre; gram and kilogram; litre and millilitre).

Teacher information

In science, a machine can be thought of as anything that can change the size or direction of a force. Levers, pulleys and gears are examples of machines.

A lever is a very simple machine. It requires a fulcrum (pivot) and a bar balancing on that fulcrum. What you need to lift (the load) is on one side of the fulcrum and the force you need to lift it (the effort) is on the other side of the fulcrum. Levers make it easier to move objects as they allow for a smaller force to be applied over a longer distance, therefore increasing the effectiveness of that force. So if you want to lift a big load with a smaller effort, the load must be *nearer* the fulcrum (pivot) than the effort is. The further the effort is from the pivot the more effective the lever.

In this case the load is the tin lid, the fulcrum is the edge of the tin and the effort is provided by the downward force from your hand on the knife. If we used a very short knife it would be harder to open the tin.

Other examples are things like scissors or pliers and anything else needed to grip or cut. The further away the force from the pivot, the more effective the machine is. Similarly, the closer the object to be cut is to the pivot (in a pair of scissors) the greater the force and it cuts better.

Gears are wheels with teeth that can either increase the speed of a machine or the force the machine exerts on the load, but not both at the same time. Gears work in exactly the same way as levers as a force multiplier.

If you put two or more wheels together and loop a rope around them you create a lifting machine called a pulley. Each time the rope wraps around the wheels, you multiply the load you can lift. If there are four wheels and the rope wraps around them, the pulley works as though four ropes are supporting the load. So you can lift four times as much. However, you have to pull the rope four times further so it seems like you are putting more effort into it when in fact you are using less effort compared to the load.

Launch pad

Give out the launch pad activity and introduce the context that they are exploring simple machines. Provide a range of machines that rely on a lever. Allow the children to work out how to operate each machine and encourage the children to formulate a question or two about these machines. Get them to record their responses on the sheet or on a learning wall.

Now pose the question: 'How does where I push make a difference to the load I can lift?' Ask them to plan a suitable investigation to answer this question. Remember, this is your base-line assessment so do not intervene at this point. If they are struggling to suggest ways to find out, they can put 'I do not know' or a '?'.

Ask the children to complete the first column of the self-assessment sheet.

Resources

A range of simple machines that use levers – good examples to use are scissors, wheelbarrow, pliers, tweezers

Long pieces of wood to act as a lever/screwdriver etc. to open a tin

Metre rulers made of wood

A tin can or triangular block to act as a pivot

Access to secondary sources

Activity 1

Target group: Years 5 and 6 who are working towards ARE.
Aim: To develop approaches to answer questions.

What to do

Ask children to explore a variety of basic lever or pulley systems. Use the basic planning mat (see Appendix) to help formulate the questions. Model one question formulation about the machine and then highlight the main question stems and connectives in the main body of the question. Allow children to brainstorm their own questions for a while using the basic planning mat and display responses on a learning wall. Using the basic question mat, ask them to develop two specific questions about the machine to answer requiring different investigative methods. Collate all the answers around the learning wall. Ask them also to think of some ways to answer their questions and record these methods on the learning wall.

Together, establish a list of scientific ways to answer a question, and cross-reference with the basic planning mat as you are doing this.

Now provide the children with a range of questions about levers and pulleys, such as:

- How does a lever work? (observation and research)
- How does a pulley work? (observation and research)
- What is the best simple machine to lift a piano? (research)
- What is the best machine to grip something tightly? (observation and research)
- What simple machines are similar to a pair of scissors? (observation and research)
- How does the number of turns in a pulley system affect the load it can lift? (observation, fair test and research)
- What common machines are levers? (research and classification)
- What common machines are pulleys? (research and classification)

Have around the room different ways to answer these questions.

Group the children and give them a specific question. Look at the options of how to answer the questions. Ask the children to match the question with the method that was used while at the same time exploring the ways to answer it. Then provide the rest of the questions related to levers and pulleys and ask them to match the question with the method.

Tips

● Ensure that some questions have multiple methods to answer them.
● Ask the children to rank the ways of finding out the answers and then make a judgement on the best way to answer the question.
● Carry this out as a group activity, encouraging talk in the investigations.

Key questions to develop the skill

● What could you do to find out this answer? Could you do something else?
● Could you think of another way to answer the question? Which way do you think is best?

Key vocabulary

Question, investigation, ideas, answers, distance, load, effort, lever, pulley, gear, pivot

Resources

Different types of simple machines: scissors/lever/pliers/tweezers

Simple pulley systems

Masses

Activity 2

Target group: Years 5 and 6 who are working at ARE.
Aim: To develop the skill of planning investigations.

What to do

Provide children with a specific question to answer relating to simple levers or pulleys requiring comparative and fair testing (see the list in Activity 1). Use the advanced planning mats to model and explore with them the variables and what they think might happen. Ask them to follow the investigation to see if they have answered the question (the focus should not be on the write-up or presentation of results as we are interested in structure of the planning).

Now provide the children with three methods based upon answering the one question. Ask them to discuss the methods and agree on which one is the best. Now using the children's input come up with a list of rules for planning a fair test investigation. Refer to the advanced planning mat to model how we identify variables. Take another question and draft a method together with the children, using the rules.

Use the advanced planning mat to formulate sentences, explaining at each point why we use this language.

Tips

- The concept of the fair test is tricky. It might require a separate teaching sequence.
- Don't get hung up on the language of variables; it is enough to refer to them as 'factors' or even 'things', just be consistent.
- For a more kinaesthetic, whole-class way to model planning use the planning posters developed by the National Strategies (see Bibliography).
- Always refer their plan back to the original question. With controlled investigations the clue to the variables is located in the question.
- Carry this out as a group activity, encouraging talk in the investigations.

Key questions to develop the skill

- What could you do to find out this answer? Could you do something else?
- Could you think of another way to answer the question? Which way do you think is best?
- What could you change in this investigation? What will you keep the same to make it fair?
- What will you measure in this investigation?

Key vocabulary

Question, investigation, ideas, answers, distance, load, effort, lever, pulley, gear, pivot

Resources

A pulley system with weights

A lever system with weights

Planning mat

The final activity

Explore again the children's plan to answer the original levers question. Ask them to annotate it, amend it, add to it or clarify the plan. If you have time, carry out the investigation.

Give out the final self-assessment sheet and ask children to complete the second column.

3 Observations, measuring and recording

Observing, measuring and recording

The skill of observing, measuring and recording evidence within 'Working scientifically' is an integral part of the 'scientific method' that can also be seen as the beginning or initial skill at the start of the scientific process (Harlen and Qualter 2015). Children are naturally inquisitive – they want to engage with the world around them and use their senses to explore it. For children this exploration is the key to gathering evidence.

Figure 3.1 shows the skills progression in the National Curriculum. As we progress through the year groups, the expectation is that the methodology of 'gathering evidence' becomes more formalised and structured and there is a shift from random observations and noticing things to seeking evidence in a purposeful way. As a consequence, the children experience a wider range of methods of collecting evidence and equipment to do this. Running alongside this is the way that the children record and present their evidence, which again becomes more formalised.

This skill set is intimately linked with the literacy and numeracy skills of the children. Therefore to secure progress, particular attention needs to be paid to their abilities in order for them to express themselves using appropriate vocabulary in the earlier stages and in the later stages utilising standard measurements and units. This, of course, might mean additional interventions are needed.

Looking at this in another way and in a bit more detail, we can gain a sense of what skills might be inherent in these steps yet are not explicitly mentioned – those that are earlier in the development and later in the development (see Figure 3.2).

Barriers to progress

Language. As previously mentioned, there is sometimes an assumption that children know how to express their observations. This is often not the case and some children need help to develop this skill. Even though qualitative observations seem to be a lower-level skill, these still require a rich vocabulary of adjectives and therefore will be dependent on the literacy levels of the children you are teaching. If the children have a limited vocabulary they may not be able to demonstrate their understanding. When children lack the vocabulary, they can resort to similes in an attempt to express what they experience. As Johnston (2009) notes, children often come up with the most random observations and similes, and a skilled teacher needs to see these for what they are – a rich source of evidence of progress.

In addition, we might, as teachers, expect observations to be expressed using subject-specific vocabulary that the child simply does not have. For example, using the terms 'non-magnetic' or 'transparent', when describing materials.

Relevance of the evidence. This is entirely dependent on the teacher and the context of the investigation that they are using. If a teacher rejects a child's observation because it seems

Lower primary Years 1 and 2

> **Observing closely, using simple equipment**
>
> **Gathering and recording data to help in answering questions**
>
> *Non-statutory guidance*: They should use simple features to compare objects, materials and living things and, with help, decide how to sort and group them, observe changes over time.
>
> They should use simple measurements and equipment (for example, hand lenses, egg timers) to gather data.

Lower Key Stage 2 Years 3 and 4

> **Taking measurements, using a range of scientific equipment, with increasing accuracy and precision, taking repeat readings when appropriate**
>
> **Gathering, recording, classifying and presenting data in a variety of ways to help in answering questions**
>
> **Recording findings using simple scientific language, drawings, labelled diagrams, keys, bar charts and tables**
>
> *Non-statutory guidance*: They should help to make decisions about what observations to make, how long to make them for and the type of simple equipment that might be used. They should learn how to use new equipment, such as data loggers, appropriately. They should collect data from their own observations and measurements, using notes, simple tables and standard units, and help to make decisions about how to record and analyse this data.

Upper Key Stage 2 Years 5 and 6

> **Making systematic and careful observations and, where appropriate, taking accurate measurements using standard units, using a range of equipment, including thermometers and data loggers**
>
> **Recording data and results of increasing complexity using scientific diagrams and labels, classification keys, tables, scatter graphs, bar and line graphs**
>
> *Non-statutory guidance*: They should make their own decisions about what observations to make, what measurements to use and how long to make them for, and whether to repeat them; choose the most appropriate equipment to make measurements and explain how to use it accurately. They should decide how to record data from a choice of familiar approaches.

Figure 3.1 Progress in ARE in the skill area of observing, measuring and recording (National Curriculum in England: Science programmes of study, 2015).

Basic skills	*Advanced skills*
Using senses/Using simple equipment	Using a range of more complex scientific equipment
Less accurate observation through less skilled use of equipment	More accurate observations through skilled use of equipment
Less precision and greater variation in observations	More precision with less variation in evidence
Using descriptive/comparative/proportional language/non-standard measurements	Using standard units in observations
Little independence in decision-making	More independence in decision-making, e.g. making choices on types of equipment, data and frequency
No repeats	Repeating measurements to increase reliability
Observing changes over time	Observing specific events in a specific time frame
Using more common measurements in context	Using less common measurements in context (e.g. force – Newtons)
Extracting information from given sources	Can independently select information sources and information to use from those sources
Recording events and descriptions in provided templates	Recording data in appropriate formats chosen by the child

Figure 3.2 Key steps in progress for gathering evidence.

random and seemingly irrelevant, the teacher risks rejecting evidence of progress and in some cases damaging the child's self-esteem, making them more reluctant to participate in future. It is therefore vital that the teacher becomes skilled at recognising an observation, even if it does not seem relevant.

Using equipment. The next step in progress for many observations is the extension of senses using equipment to make the observation (Harlen and Qualter 2015). The skill of the child in using this equipment is crucial. Some may not have encountered a set of scales before, while some may be used to digital equipment whereas you are using analogue. Never assume the children will recognise the equipment or know how to use it, always check. This can, in part, be resolved by introducing the equipment to the pupils at an early stage, encouraging play and finding out what they know about the equipment. You will also need to be aware that the equipment can, in itself, become the focus of the exploration rather than the observation. It is important to note as well if any of your children have motor skill issues as this can limit progress if the observation is dependent on using a piece of equipment.

Numeracy. Using equipment for observation is sometimes dependent on the numeracy skills of the pupils. It is not automatic that children will have the same level of literacy and numeracy skills (think of yourself: are you as confident in maths as you are in English?). Some digital scales read to one decimal point, others to two. Some stopwatches measure in hundredths of a second, some in whole seconds. Will the children know this? Can the children count in hundredths or even thousandths?

Accuracy and precision. We expect children in Years 3 and 4 to work with increasing precision and accuracy. In order for a child to select a piece of equipment they must have a basic understanding of these concepts. This is a notoriously difficult set of concepts to get across, partly because conceptually they are challenging and partly because there is disagreement or variation in the definitions used by different organisations (exam boards etc.). This is discussed at length, along with the development of some useful definitions and examples, by Gott et al. (2015) and a useful set of definitions is provided by the work of the ASE (2010) in the guide *The Language of Measurement: Terminology Used in School Science Investigations* (see Figure 3.3).

For most children at primary age this step in progress is not about the terminology, it is about the practical experience, for example comparing their data against another person's or group's when measuring and interpreting and realising it is not the same. The key step in this progress is to discuss and explore why measurements might vary and what they can practically do to reduce this variation.

Qualitative observations are observations that are descriptive (describing the quality of something in size, appearance, value etc.) and although often seen as 'simple' they can be quite sophisticated and are affected by the vocabulary of the children.

Quantitative observations are observations relating to the number, quantity or measurements of an object. They therefore are dependent on the mathematical skills of the children you are teaching. For example, in the areas of number and measurement if a child cannot count up to 100 they might struggle to use metre rulers to measure.

Accuracy describes the difference between the measurement you make and the true value, so if something is more accurate it is closer to the true value.

Precision describes the variation from the mean when you measure the same thing repeatedly with the same device. A reading or result is said to be more precise if there is little variation between readings and the mean value using the same device and the same person doing the measuring.

Quantitative data can be more or less accurate and precise. In science investigations we aim for accuracy and precision. If there is a lot of variation between readings then it is less precise. It is possible for something to be very precise but not very accurate. It also follows that something can also be very accurate but not very precise. You can increase accuracy by using appropriate equipment and scales, but it also depends on how that equipment is read by the scientist using it.

Although not required at primary level, it is important that teachers understand the following terms:

Repeatability: This is the ability for you to replicate your results using the same equipment and methods.

Reproducibility: This is the ability for someone else to replicate your results using the same method and equipment.

Based on Gott et al. (2015)

Figure 3.3 Information for the teacher.

Timing. It is important you know the time implications of any particular enquiry. An investigation that is observation over time requires just that. Biological processes and systems in particular need time to yield observations and this can be from hours to months (changes in trees over seasons for example).

Moreover, as Johnston (2009) notes, children need time to talk, to discuss their observations and process contradictory evidence. If this time is not given, then children might not make conceptual progress.

The teacher's skills. It is important that you try out the investigations prior to teaching. Put yourself in the children's shoes and carry out your own observations to see the range of evidence available for any particular enquiry. More importantly when dealing with older children, ensure you have a clear understanding of what affects the degree of trust in evidence in any specific investigation.

General suggestions for the teacher

1 Provide multiple opportunities, both formal and informal, to observe. This could involve providing contextual artefacts and examples prior to the topic being studied either in the form of a display or bench in the class or going beyond the classroom to objects or events outside.
2 Provide the contextual language if children are struggling to articulate their observations or have limited vocabulary.
3 Provide number lines if children are struggling to articulate their measurements.
4 Provide examples of nonsense observations and measurements that all profess to measure the same thing. Ask how useful these are and how we could make them more useful.
5 Provide groups of children something to measure, such as a length of string. Give them an object to measure it with like a toy animal or an orange and ask them to quantify it and then share it with the rest of the class – for example, 'My string is fifteen lions long.' Question how useful this is.
6 Focus on the skill specifically and make the children aware of this, either through shared objectives or dedicated 'observing time' in every science lesson.
7 Extend skills in observation to include more novel things to observe and different equipment to observe with. This might require more specialist equipment but can equally be possible with equipment that is more freely available such as digital cameras and ICT for making slideshows or comic books.
8 Provide opportunities for children to talk about and share their observations with each other and you.
9 Model the correct use of instruments that can be used to help in observations, such as hand lenses, digital cameras, rulers, measuring cylinders, time pieces such as stopwatches, jugs, thermometers and probes.
10 Using a suitable format, ask a group of pupils to describe how to use a particular type of equipment to another group in the class so that they can use it.
11 Spend some time gathering evidence and making observations over extended periods of time with an appropriate investigation – for example, growing plants.
12 Identify key questions that will challenge selected pupils and get them to think about what they are doing and why they are doing it.
13 Provide children with an incorrect method of how to measure something and then let them explore and correct the method.

14 Use card matching games – for example, matching an observation value with an object and a piece of equipment.

15 Use games such as 'Bull's eye' (Goldsworthy and Ponchaud 2007) to make more demanding concepts, such as precision and accuracy, more accessible.

16 Use an observation planning board/mat to help develop language, skills and numbers.

Questions to help develop observing, measuring and recording

What is that?

What do you see?

What colour/size/shape is that?

Can you describe that for me?

How big/small is that?

How heavy/light is that?

How is that different from that?

How is that the same as that?

What words could you use to describe what is happening there?

What words would better describe that?

What could you use to measure that?

What do you want to use to measure that?

How does that work?

How do you use that equipment?

What units do we use to measure that?

How useful are those measurements?

How could you improve the way that you measured that?

Why is that measurement different to that one?

Is that accurate?

How could you make your reading more accurate?

Why is that not accurate?

Whose measurements were most accurate? Why?

Why have they got a different result to you, even though they used the same equipment?

Why did you use that?

If you were to measure it again, would you get the same result? Why?

What is the best way to show what you have found out?

What is a table of results?

There follows three contexts to explore and develop the skills of raising questions, predicting and planning which directly relate to the new programme of study. These are:

Years 1 and 2 – Investigating the school garden

Years 3 and 4 – Investigating sound

Years 5 and 6 – Investigating fossils.

Measuring, observing and recording

Years 1 and 2: Investigating the school garden

Working scientifically

Working at age-related expectations (Years 1 and 2)

Observing closely, using simple equipment – for example, observe changes over time, use simple measurements and equipment.

Guidance (non-statutory): They should use simple measurements and equipment (for example, hand lenses, egg timers) to gather data.

Working above age-related expectations (Years 3 and 4)

Making systematic and careful observations and, where appropriate, taking accurate measurements using standard units, using a range of equipment, including thermometers and data loggers.

Guidance (non-statutory): They should help to make decisions about what observations to make, how long to make them for and the type of simple equipment that might be used. They should learn how to use new equipment, such as data loggers, appropriately. They should collect data from their own observations and measurements.

Years 1 and 2 context

Working at age-related expectations

Identify and name a variety of common wild and garden plants, including deciduous and evergreen trees.

Identify and describe the basic structure of a variety of common flowering plants, including trees.

Mathematics

Working at age-related expectations (Years 1 and 2)

Number
Count to and across 100, forwards and backwards, beginning with 0 or 1, or from any given number.

Count, read and write numbers to 100 in numerals; count in multiples of twos, fives and tens.

Given a number, identify one more and one less.

Identify and represent numbers using objects and pictorial representations including the number line, and use the language of: equal to, more than, less than (fewer), most, least.

Read and write numbers from 1 to 20 in numerals and words.

Measurement

Measure and begin to record the following: lengths and heights.

Compare, describe and solve practical problems for: lengths and heights (for example, long/short, longer/shorter, tall/short, double/half).

Teacher information

Within this context you need to be aware of the distinction between what is considered to be a 'wild' plant and what a 'garden' plant is. The distinction is often made using the term 'weed' as often natural plants found in the garden are unwanted. However, there has been a trend towards creating 'wild' areas in a garden. For example in the UK, natural wild plants found in gardens tend to be 'weeds' like daisies, buttercups, ragworts, plantains, clovers, nettles, rose-bay willow, herbs and grasses. The trend towards creating artificial 'meadows' has led to other plants like cornflowers, Scabious sp, etc. being planted.

Popular garden plants such as pansies, violas, petunias, roses, chrysanthemums and dahlias are used for colour. Typical garden plants will depend on the taste of the gardener and the time of year. They tend to be:

- **Annuals:** flowering plants that flower once in a year and die.
- **Perennials:** flowering plants that flower and die back year after year.

The common vocabulary to describe the most basic structure of a common herbaceous flowering plant is root, stem, leaf, flower, bud.

One other common garden plant is a **shrub**. Shrubs are larger plants that tend to have woody growth and get bigger each year. Shrubs commonly seen in gardens include buddleia, lilac, hedges such as privet etc.

Trees are larger plants that have a woody 'trunk' with a layer of material called 'bark' around it. Some trees make obvious flowers, others do not. Trees are generally classified using the following:

- **Evergreens:** trees that do not lose their leaves any time of the year.
- **Deciduous:** trees that shed their leaves once a year and have new growth in the spring.

The common vocabulary for trees is root, trunk, branch, twig, leaf, flower, crown, seed, fruit.

Launch pad

Introduce the context: you want to know about the different plants in the school garden.

Give out the launch pad activity. If access is available, go on a garden nature trail or around the school grounds and look at the variety of plants and trees that are found. While moving around the garden, start engaging children in conversations about what they see. If possible, encourage them to collect some leaves, seeds etc. (emphasise care for living things), take photographs, make sketches or drawings.

When back in the classroom introduce them to some more stimulus materials, maybe in the form of a 'garden bench' somewhere in the classroom where plants, leaves, flowers, seeds etc. are kept in order to stimulate questions and discussions. Include some observation equipment such as hand lenses or hand-held digital cameras that they can use if they want.

Explain that you want them to communicate/tell you what they have observed or noted in a display about the plants. They can draw and label, or stick and label, any images and words about the leaves and plants either on the launch pad sheet or on a learning wall.

Be active in looking for their observations and taking notes on any child you wish to focus on to note their base-line. Do not give the children any help at this point as this will be your base-line assessment. Give out the self-assessment sheet and ask children to complete the first column.

Resources

A variety of plant materials

Clear plastic bags or trays for collecting materials

General stationery/poster materials

Digital cameras

Hand lenses/magnifying glasses

Rulers

Activity 1

Target group: Years 1 and 2 who are working at ARE.
Aim: To develop the idea of qualitative observations.

What to do

Ask the children to look at a variety of trees and make observations based on their senses, i.e. what they can see, smell, hear and touch. If you want you can use the question, 'How are trees different to each other?'

Give out and refer to the basic observation mat and look at the box titled, 'My observational words'. Review with the children the words that they could use to describe the plants. These are all observations. Allow them to explore and record in the 'what I observed' box. Allow for other words and similes. Encourage not just words but drawings and any object they want to stick on the sheet.

Conclude the activity by emphasising the word 'observation' and that we can use observations to answer questions. Go back to the original question, 'How are the trees different?', and challenge them to use their words in response.

Tips

- At this age we are looking for observations of similarities and differences between the plants. This will generally come from using observational language and may include early 'quantifying' statements, such as bigger or smaller and some simple measurements such as length of leaf etc.
- Closer observations will come from closer inspection of trees such as their leaves, bark or seeds. Suitable equipment might be simple hand lenses.

Key questions to develop the skill

- What is that?
- What colour is it?
- What does it look like?
- What does the leaf look like?
- What is the shape of the leaf? Describe its shape.
- How is the leaf divided?
- What words could I use to describe that leaf?
- How is that leaf different to that leaf? How is that leaf similar to that leaf?
- What is the shape of that tree? How is that shape different from that shape? How can you tell?
- What did you use to make that observation?
- What can you smell?
- What does that feel like?

Encourage the use of some specific observations related to the key vocabulary below and use questions to isolate particular words.

Key vocabulary

Size, colour, number, texture, smell, shape, taste, sound

Size words: long, short, narrow, wide, big, small, medium

Colour words: brown, grey, green, orange, red, blue, black, white

Specific leaf words: lobed, blade, saw, divided

Specific plant words: stem, leaf, flower, roots, trunk, branch, bark

Shape words: box, round, cone, triangle, square, rectangle

Texture words: rough, smooth, spikey

Smell words: sweet, woody

Activity 2

Target group: Years 1 and 2 who are working above ARE.
Aim: To develop the idea of quantitative observations.

What to do

Children are to look at a variety of plants in the classroom and make observations based on measurements. If you want, you can ask the question, 'How can we tell these plants apart?'

Look at the basic observation mat. Allow them to look at the observation words and equipment section of the mat. Encourage them at first to make qualitative observations and record them under the section 'What I have observed'. Then pose a question that requires a quantitative answer such as: Which one has the most leaves? Which one has the biggest leaves?

Use the section 'My observation numbers' and encourage the children to decide what to count and measure. They can record what they measured such as length of leaf, number of leaves etc. in the central space, either in a template of their own design or one you have provided.

Tips

- The key step is to move children into making more quantifiable observations.
- Allow the children time to talk about this while you eavesdrop.
- If children get stuck on qualitative observations, guide them to things to measure, and explain that measuring things is a good observation to make, especially when things change or look different, as it can help us tell things apart.
- In this investigation the key measurements are 'number', e.g. leaves/flowers; size: length/width/height; number: length/width in cm or mm.
- Provide scaffolds to record results – use simple tables with rows labelled plant 1, 2 etc. (or named plant if they have identified the plant) and columns with the other variables such as number of leaves/size of leaf etc.

Key questions to develop the skill

- How many leaves/flowers does it have?
- How big is it? What is its length? What is its width? How tall is it?
- How is that plant different to that plant?
- How is that plant similar to that plant?
- How big is its leaf? How wide is its leaf? How many parts does the leaf have?
- What are you going to use to measure that?
- What is that measured in?

Resources

Rulers, in mm, cm, m

Graph paper (please note that mathematically 'area' is conceptually advanced so you will need to judge if the children can cope with this)

Digital scales

The final activity

For the final activity reissue the original launch pad task. You will now go back out into the garden or on a nature walk and ask the children to use their observational skills to describe what they are seeing.

Key questions to guide your dialogue are as follows:

- What are you looking at?
- What observations do you want to use?
- What words are you using?
- What are you measuring?

Ask the children to add to and annotate their word mat with any other information that they have found out:

- key observation words
- key measurements
- key equipment they would use.

Present them with their display and ask them to amend it or add to it (if time allows they can make a new display).

Give out the self-assessment sheet and ask children to complete the second column.

Observing, measuring and recording

Years 3+ 4: Investigating sound

Working scientifically

Working towards age-related expectations

Observing closely, using simple equipment such as magnifying glasses and hand lenses.

Guidance (non-statutory): They should use simple measurements and equipment (for example, hand lenses, egg timers) to gather data.

Working at age-related expectations

Making systematic and careful observations and, where appropriate, taking accurate measurements using standard units, using a range of equipment, including thermometers and data loggers.

Guidance (non-statutory): They should help to make decisions about what observations to make, how long to make them for and the type of simple equipment that might be used. They should learn how to use new equipment, such as data loggers, appropriately. They should collect data from their own observations and measurements.

Working above age-related expectations

Taking measurements, using a range of scientific equipment, with increasing accuracy and precision, taking repeat readings when appropriate.

Guidance (non-statutory): They should make their own decisions about what observations to make, what measurements to use and how long to make them for, and whether to repeat them; choose the most appropriate equipment to make measurements and explain how to use it accurately.

Years 3 and 4 context: Sound

Working at age-related expectations

Pupils should be taught to:

- identify how sounds are made, associating some of them with something vibrating
- recognise that vibrations from sounds travel through a medium to the ear
- find patterns between the pitch of a sound and features of the object that produced it
- find patterns between the volume of a sound and the strength of the vibrations that produced it
- recognise that sounds get fainter as the distance from the sound source increases.

Mathematics

Working at age-related expectations (Year 3)

Number
Count to and across 100, forwards and backwards, beginning with 0 or 1, or from any given number.

Count, read and write numbers to 100 in numerals; count in multiples of twos, fives and tens.

Given a number, identify one more and one less.

Identify and represent numbers using objects and pictorial representations including the number line, and use the language of: equal to, more than, less than (fewer), most, least.

Read and write numbers from 1 to 20 in numerals and words.

Measurement
Measure and begin to record the following: lengths and heights.

Compare, describe and solve practical problems for: lengths and heights (for example, long/short, longer/shorter, tall/short, double/half).

Teacher information

Sound is a means of transferring energy from one place to another through vibrations. If something can vibrate then it can transfer sound energy. The substance that a sound wave travels through is called its medium. This can be a solid, liquid or gas. Contrary to popular belief we can hear through all mediums.

Sound waves can vary in their loudness (amplitude) and their pitch (frequency) and this is dependent on how large the vibrations are and how often they occur. If a sound wave has a high frequency it will be high pitched. If a sound wave has a large amplitude it will have a greater volume. A sound wave does not need to have a large amplitude in order for it to be high pitched and vice versa.

Objects make sound waves by vibrating. In the case of musical instruments, a percussion instrument vibrates once it has been hit. This in turn vibrates the air and transfers the sound wave. By varying the tension in the surface or the material it is made from we can create different frequency vibrations and different notes in a percussive instrument.

A string instrument makes sound by the strings vibrating after they have been plucked or hit. This in turn vibrates the air and transfers the sound. By varying the tension in the strings we can create different frequency vibrations and different notes in a stringed instrument.

A wind instrument makes sound by the air contained inside it vibrating, usually by blowing into or across it. By varying the volume of air we can create different frequency vibrations and different notes in a wind instrument.

Launch pad

Give out the launch pad activity sheet. Pose the question: How can we change a sound?

Provide the children with a basic stringed instrument. Ask them to make different sounds with the instrument. What did they do? How did they make the sound? Move them on and ask how the sound changed, what they did and how they knew it had changed.

Ask the children to record their ideas on a poster or on the launch pad sheet. Since this is your base-line assessment they can work together on the noise but not on the poster. Do not give the children any help at this point as this will be your base-line assessment – you are looking for any observations that they make.

Give the children the self-assessment sheet and ask them to complete the first try column.

Resources

Provide the children with simple equipment that they can use to observe like hand lenses, binoculars, digital cameras, digital sound recorders and rulers

A basic stringed instrument

Activity 1

Target group: Years 3 and 4 who are working towards ARE.
Aim: To develop the skill of qualitative observations.

What to do

Ask the children to work at making a variety of sounds. If you want you can use the question: 'How can we make sounds with these objects?' Provide them with simple equipment that they can use to make their observations like hand lenses, digital cameras and digital sound recorders.

Give out the basic observation mat. Referring to the mat, look at the options for what they could observe and how they could observe it. Use text marking to select what they will do. Look at the box titled 'My observational words'. Review with the children the words that they used to describe their objects and how they made the sound. These are all observations. Record them in the 'What I observed' box. Allow for other words and similes. Encourage not just words but drawings and any object they want to stick on the sheet.

Conclude the activity by emphasising the word 'observation' and that we can use observations to answer questions. Go back to the original question, 'How can we make sounds with these objects?', and challenge the children to use their words.

Tips

- At this age we are looking for observations of similarities and differences between the objects and the sounds they make. This will generally come from using observational language and may include early 'quantifying' statements such as bigger or smaller and some simple measurements such as length of the elastic band etc.
- More detailed observations will come from closer inspection of the objects such as the elastic band or the skin of a drum to see the vibrations.

Key questions to develop the skill

- How did you make the noise? What did you use? Can you show me what you did?
- How did the object affect the type of noise? Was that noise different to that noise?
- What was the difference between that noise and that noise?
- How could you make that noise different?

Key vocabulary

Quantity words: long, short, narrow, wide, big, small, medium, loud, soft, high, low

Texture words: rough, smooth, woolly, fluffy, hard, soft

Verbs: hit, pluck, drum, scratch, drop

Sound words: bang, boom, buzz, crash, crackling, crunching, muffled, noisy, pop, quietly, rustle, sloshing, softly, loudly, tinkle

Activity 2

Target group: Years 3 and 4 who are working at ARE.
Aim: To develop the skill of quantitative observations.

What to do

Provide the children with musical instruments such as drums, tambourines, triangles, guitars, banjos, flutes etc. to represent the different generation of sound. Provide them with simple equipment that they can use to observe such as hand lenses, digital cameras, digital sound recorders, sound meters.

Allocate the children different instruments and then pose the question to challenge the pupils:

- How could I make the sound LOUDER/SOFTER? (How can I get a different amplitude?)
- How could I make the sound HIGHER/LOWER? (How can I get a different pitch note?)

Use the sections 'My measurements' and 'My equipment' on the advanced observation mat and encourage them to record what they measured such as length of string, number of strikes, number of turns etc. and how they measured it. In the central space, either in a template of their own design or one you have provided, they can record their observations.

Introduce the children to a sound meter (if you haven't already). This will measure the amplitude (loudness) of the sound.

The key step is to move children into making more quantifiable observations. Allow the children time to talk about this while you eavesdrop. Provide scaffolds to record results – use simple tables with rows labelled. Move around the room talking to pupils. Encourage and challenge the use of mathematical skills through questioning to quantify their observations.

Tips

- Allow the children time to explore and work together.
- If children get stuck on qualitative observations, guide the children to things to measure, and explain that measuring things is a good observation to make, especially when things change or look different as it can help us tell things apart.
- The challenge now is to move into quantitative observations using different equipment. In this context the focus will be on:
  - For string instruments: increasing/decreasing the length of the string/ruler to produce a higher or lower pitch note.
  - For wind instruments: increasing/decreasing the length of the wind chamber or increasing/decreasing the volume of the chamber.
  - For percussion instruments: increasing/decreasing the tension of the skin/increasing or decreasing the force used to create the note.

Key questions to develop the skill

- How many turns did you make to make it tighter?
- What is the length of the string?
- How hard did you hit that?
- How far did you drop it?

Resources

Rulers: inches, mm, cm, m

Digital scales

Hand lenses

Stopwatches

Sound meter

Activity 3

Target group: Years 3 and 4 who are working above ARE.
Aim: To develop the concepts of accuracy and precision.

What to do

The children will be working with data that differs, even though they have all done the same experiment with the same equipment. If you want, you can ask the question: 'Which instrument makes the loudest sound?' Play a number of instruments and ask the children to judge the amplitude (how loud the sound was) and then rank the instruments. Arrange the groups thus:

- Group 1: just use their ears
- Group 2: their ears and a written decibel scale
- Group 3: a decibel meter (or a data logger).

Once all the results are in, use the advanced observation mat to record their results. Compare each group's results and make the point that they all heard the same sounds but there were differences in their observations. Introduce the terminology of 'precise' and 'accurate'.

The more accurate group were group 3 as they had a device that was closest to the actual level. Now ask them to repeat their readings. But this time allow the groups that didn't have the decibel meter to use it. There should now be more consistency between the groups, but there will still be variations.

The findings are still not precise because there is still variation, even though the same equipment has been used. Discuss with them why this might be the case (e.g. some groups held the decibel meter further away from the sound source).

We can make things precise by repeating the measurement until we get similar readings from accurate readings using suitable equipment (and the same person).

Use the advanced observation mat to express how to make an observation more accurate and, if possible, more precise. Complete the section on 'My tips'.

Tips

- This investigation is very demanding cognitively and numerically and should only be used with those children you feel can cope with the demand.
- This activity will need to be pitched very carefully if you want to develop the idea of precision (at this stage it might be enough to develop the idea of accuracy).

Key questions to develop the skill

- Were there differences between you and the other groups?
- Why was there a difference?
- What happened when you all tried using the decibel meter? Were your results closer to the other groups' results?
- Why might this have happened?

The final activity

Re-introduce the original launch pad: How can we change a sound?

Re-issue their original poster. Ask the children to amend it by answering the questions again.

Provide the children with a variety of objects, musical instruments and artefacts and ask them to make music. Provide them with simple equipment that they can use to make their observations such as hand lenses, binoculars, digital cameras, digital sound recorders and rulers, and if you can make it available, a decibel meter or a data logger with a decibel meter on it.

Ask the children to complete the second column of the self-assessment sheet.

Observing, measuring and recording

Years 5 and 6: Investigating fossils

Working scientifically

Working towards age-related expectations

Observing closely, using simple equipment such as magnifying glasses and hand lenses.

Making systematic and careful observations and, where appropriate, taking accurate measurements using standard units, using a range of equipment, including thermometers and data loggers.

Guidance (non-statutory): The children should help to make decisions about what observations to make, how long to make them for and the type of simple equipment that might be used. They should learn how to use new equipment, such as data loggers, appropriately. They should collect data from their own observations and measurements.

Working at age-related expectations

Taking measurements, using a range of scientific equipment, with increasing accuracy and precision, taking repeat readings when appropriate.

Guidance (non-statutory): They should make their own decisions about what observations to make, what measurements to use and how long to make them for, and whether to repeat them; choose the most appropriate equipment to make measurements and explain how to use it accurately.

Years 5 and 6 context

Working at age-related expectations

Recognise that living things have changed over time and that fossils provide information about living things that inhabited Earth millions of years ago.

Identify how animals and plants are adapted to suit their environment in different ways and that adaptation may lead to evolution.

Mathematics

Working at age-related expectations (Year 5)

Number
Read, write, order and compare numbers to at least 1,000,000 and determine the value of each digit.

Count forwards or backwards in steps of powers of 10 for any given number up to 1,000,000.

Measurement
Convert between different units of metric measure (for example, kilometre and metre; centimetre and metre; centimetre and millimetre; gram and kilogram; litre and millilitre).

Teacher information

Fossils are the remains of organisms that were once alive. Most fossils are found in types of rock called *sedimentary rock*. Sedimentary rock is rock that has been made from sediment, like sand or mud. Over time, these small pieces are compressed (squashed together) as more layers of sediment are laid on top of them. Eventually, they are compressed into sedimentary rock. The deeper the layer of rock, the older it is. The closer to the surface, the more recent it is.

Fossils are either made when an imprint is left or the original parts are gradually replaced by minerals and after a long period of time can form rock. Fossils usually have the same shape as the original item (unless it has been really squashed and distorted), but their colour, mass and density depends on what minerals it was made from. Fossils are usually heavier than the real thing since they are basically rock.

The most common fossils are fossils of bones, teeth, claws and track marks. Less common are things like skin and feathers, leaves of plants and egg shells.

Launch pad

Give out the launch pad activity sheet and pose the question: 'How can we tell these fossils apart?'

Ask children to 'observe' and 'note' anything about the fossils that they could use to tell the fossils apart. Ask the children to record their observations in a suitable format and to explain how they made their observations accurate.

Do not give the children any help at this point as this will be your base-line assessment. Circulate and eavesdrop on the children's conversations; ask questions but do not interfere.

Ask the children to complete the first column of the self-assessment sheet.

Resources

Each table will need:

Bag of fossils

Fake bones, shells

Pictures of fossils

Measuring cylinders, digital scales, analogue scales, Newton meters, rulers, protractors, tape measures, hand lenses, magnifiers

Graph paper

Activity 1

Target group: Years 5 and 6 who are working towards ARE.
Aim: To develop the skill of quantitative observations.

What to do

Introduce the context that the fossil detectives have found lots of organisms called trilobites in the same place. Provide children with the 'Investigating fossils' support sheet. Pose the challenge that the fossil detectives need to tell the trilobite fossils apart. Flash up or give out the image of the trilobite body map. Challenge the children that it is not enough just to describe them in this case.

Now ask the children to **choose/decide** what they think is the best thing to measure and refine their responses into three categories.

Use the advanced observation mat and the section 'My measurements' and encourage them to record what they have measured and what they used to measure it. They should record their results in the central space, either in a template of their own design or one you have provided.

Size of head

Size of eyes; number of eyes; shape of eyes

Length of body; width of body; number of segments in body

Number of spines on head; number of spines on thorax; number of spines on tail

Length of spines on head; length of spines on thorax; length of spines on tail

Tips

- Provide scaffolds to record results – use simple tables (you can use the 'precise and accurate observations' support sheet).
- If children get stuck on qualitative observations, guide them to things to measure, and explain that measuring things is a good observation to make, especially when things change or look different, as it can help us tell things apart.

- Move around the room talking to pupils. Encourage and challenge the use of mathematical skills through questioning, to quantify their observations.
- The children could well come up with mass or 'how heavy' it is. They can't measure this with the drawings so therefore, if possible, pose the question (and show a real example if you have one), 'If I had a real trilobite fossil here what else could I measure?' Allow them to handle the fossils. Once you have obtained 'weight' or 'mass' from the children illustrate measuring it and the units we could use: mass/weight; using scales in g/kg. It is important to recognise that this is perhaps not the best context to explore mass as a measurement. To try to avoid confusion, discuss with them that we are not actually measuring the mass of the trilobite but its fossil, and that this will depend not only on its size but also the material it is composed of. The point is to encourage the idea that mass is another measurement we can use to tell things apart (if relevant).

Key questions to develop the skill

- How many eyes, segments, spins does it have?
- How big is it? What is its length? What is its width? What shall we use to measure it?
- Shall we measure it in: mm or cm, g or kg?
- How is that fossil different to that fossil? How is that fossil similar to that fossil?
- Can you use the same measurement to tell these two trilobites apart?

Key vocabulary

Spines, head, eyes, thorax, abdomen, tail

Activity 2

Target group: Years 5 and 6 who are working at ARE.
Aim: To develop the concepts of accuracy and precision.

What to do

The children will be working with data that differs, even though they have all done the same experiment with the same equipment.

Arrange the children in groups of four. Provide each group with some fake plastic bones/ fossils from the launch pad activity. Give half the groups rulers that only measure in cm and spring scales that have both g and N on them. Give the other half of the group rulers that measure in mm as well as cm and digital scales that measure in g to 2dp.

Ask each member of the group to measure the length and mass of the bones and record their results without conferring on the advanced observation mat. (You can provide a recording template if you want or you can use the 'precise and accurate observations' support sheet.)

Once all the groups have discussed their observations ask one group to swap fossils and equipment with another group (the key here is to know which group is swapping with which group). Highlight the similarities between the measurements, for example there is a wide variation between the bones that were measured using the spring scales and the cm ruler and between members of the same group. There is greater similarity between those groups using the digital scales and mm rulers.

Introduce the terminology 'precise' and 'accurate'. We can make things more accurate by using more sophisticated equipment like digital scales and mm rulers. We can make things precise by repeating the measurement until we get similar readings from the equipment. You can do this with the right equipment and repeating your measurement and using the same person to measure.

Ask the children to complete the 'My tips for accuracy and precision' on their advanced observation mats.

Tips

- Ensure all the children take measurements.
- By this stage most children should be able to record results in their own templates, but have templates available (the emphasis is not on presentation).
- This investigation is very demanding cognitively and numerically and should only be used with those children you feel can cope with the demand.
- This activity will need to be pitched carefully if you want to develop the idea of precision.

Key questions to develop the skill

- Did the type of equipment you used make a difference to the observation you made?
- Were there differences in your group when you all observed the same fossil with the same equipment?
- Were there differences between your measurements and the other groups when you observed the same fossil with the same equipment?

Move around the room and eavesdrop the conversations – if needed, ask questions to improve dialogue.

Resources

Bones, fossils, fake bones

Rulers that measure in cm and mm

Rulers that only measure in cm

Analogue scales that measure in g and/or Newtons

Digital scales that measure in g to 1 or 2dp

The final activity

For the final activity, you will repeat the original launch pad task. Ask the children the question: 'How can we tell these fossils apart?' Invite them to 'observe' and 'note' anything about the fossils that they could use to tell the fossils apart. Ask the children to record their observations in a suitable format and to explain how they made their observations accurate.

Ask the children to complete the second column of the self-assessment sheet.

Resources

Each table will need:

Bag of fossils

Pictures of fossils

Measuring cylinders, digital scales, analogue scales, Newton meters, rulers, protractors, tape measures, hand lenses, magnifiers

Graph paper

4   Interpreting, analysing and concluding

Interpreting, analysing and concluding (making conclusions in investigations)

This skill area encourages children to move beyond describing and reporting what they have found out to consider what it might mean. To do this children need to be encouraged to reflect on their original question, identify what evidence (if any) can be used to answer the question, spot patterns (or be confident enough to say if there is no pattern), understand what those patterns might mean, all using scientific understanding and vocabulary, and then use them to answer their question.

Figure 4.1 shows the skills progression in the National Curriculum in England: Science programmes of study. How children progress in this skill area is intimately linked to their conceptual understanding of the science within the topic and how the evidence is presented. There is also inevitably an element of evaluation that comes with analysis since the analysis can often lead to a discussion of why we cannot make a conclusion or why we might refute the idea being investigated.

Looking at this in another way and in a bit more detail, we can gain a sense of what skills might be inherent in these steps and yet are not explicitly mentioned, and those that are earlier in the development and later in the development (see Figure 4.2).

Lower primary Years 1 and 2	**Use observations and ideas to suggest answers to questions** *Non-statutory guidance*: With guidance, they should begin to notice patterns and relationships. They should ask people questions and use simple secondary sources to find answers.
Lower Key Stage 2 Years 3 and 4	**Use results to draw simple conclusions, make predictions for new values, suggest improvements and raise further questions** **Use straightforward scientific evidence to answer questions or to support their findings** *Non-statutory guidance*: With help, pupils should look for changes, patterns, similarities and differences in their data in order to draw simple conclusions and answer questions.
Upper Key Stage 2 Years 5 and 6	**Report and present findings from enquiries, including conclusions, causal relationships and explanations of, and degree of trust in, results in oral and written forms such as displays and other presentations** **Identify scientific evidence that has been used to support or refute ideas or arguments** *Non-statutory guidance*: They should look for different causal relationships in their data and identify evidence that refutes or supports their ideas.

Figure 4.1 Progress in ARE in the skill area of reporting, analysing and concluding (National Curriculum in England: Science programmes of study 2015).

Basic skills	Advanced skills
Orally reporting on what they found out	Using the different ways to present evidence including numerical data and complex graphs/charts to analyse their data
Can identify and use a simple piece of evidence such as an observation to try to answer a question	Interpret data in a variety of formats to answer a question and a range of evidence to make a conclusion
Using simple everyday language to communicate what their evidence might mean	Use scientific concepts and language in the context of the investigation to explain what their evidence means
Basic patterns identified but not discussed and not used to answer the question	Patterns and differences are identified, causality is established, for example 'As I did this … this happened'
Vague and incomplete statements are made relating to the evidence	Complete statements made that incorporate specific evidence within a conclusion
Accepts but does not question the evidence generated in an investigation	Starting to use the ideas of 'accuracy', 'fairness' and 'precision' to discuss to what extent they can trust their evidence
	Structure clearly shows attempts to describe the pattern, make a concluding statement and explain the statement

Figure 4.2 A model of progress for reporting and analysing evidence.

Barriers to progress

Limiting the exploration to collecting and describing the data. An example would be a child looking at where woodlice are found. If the child reports they found eight woodlice under a stone this is a description only of the evidence. A pattern could only be established if they compared this evidence with other evidence collected within the investigation and if, for example, they didn't find woodlice in light, dry places or they found more woodlice in another dark, damp place such as under a log.

Not answering the question. If the children are not directed back to the original question this misses the point of the investigation. Therefore the first question a teacher should ask is 'Have you answered the question?' From that point the children can say 'yes' or 'no' and then go on to explain why, using their data.

How the data is presented. If children do not know what to look for when data is presented they can miss the patterns. It is thus important to understand the developmental level of the children in numeracy, particularly graph work. Children can sometimes have issues in the following areas:

- looking at the graph as a picture rather than a set of individual data points
- translating what they see into a verbal description or written statement

- actually using the graph to answer their original question
- interpreting just small sections of the graph that look like they are 'correct'
- reading the scales incorrectly.

Not being aware of patterns. As Harlen and Qualter (2015) note, children sometimes implicitly use patterns from their evidence without actually realising they have done so. Teachers must ensure that they are aware they have done so and use the relevant language to help them understand what they have done. This is making unconscious thought conscious. They can then go on to discussing a whole range of patterns within context.

Time. If children do not have the time to discuss, reflect on and revisit evidence, they might miss the pattern within and, in some instances, the whole point of an investigation.

Language. If the children do not have the literacy skills to be able to express relationships and patterns in evidence, then progress will be limited. For example, to express causality they will need to appreciate that when one thing is changed another thing happens. Then they will need appropriate sentence structures to be able to express this. The point is that if we expect a conclusion to be framed in a certain way we need to teach the way we expect it to be framed. An example of this is the use of 'connective words' such as 'therefore' – these are not commonly used in everyday speech but are needed to express causality.

Causality (also known as **causal link**) is the relationship between an event (the *cause*) and a second event (the *effect*), where the first event is believed to be responsible for the second.

When expressing causality we usually look for a connection between one variable being changed (the independent variable) and the result (the dependent variable). For example, if an elastic band is stretched by pulling it, the cause is the pull and the stretch is the effect. An example of a causal statement might be: 'The harder I pull the bigger the stretch.'

A **conclusion** is reached by interpreting the evidence. Simpler conclusions involve just an answer to the question; more complex conclusions involve a statement that answers an original question, using the evidence collected to provide a reason for their answer.

Figure 4.3 Information for the teacher.

Suggestions for the teacher

1   Unless you want the focus to be on the means to collect evidence or presenting the evidence then you will need to plan the experience so that it does not stop at these points. This will only address part of the skill area and can affect the pace of the investigation.
2   Always refer the evidence back to the original question or prediction. It is therefore useful to have the original question or prediction prominently displayed.
3   Provide sets of data where the variables are explicit in the presentation (a clearly labelled table) and ask the children to formulate the original question that was asked just from the data.
4   Provide sample evidence and the question it was seeking to answer and ask if the evidence could be used to answer the question (be sure to include irrelevant data).
5   Provide sets of data separate to sets of conclusions and ask the children to match the evidence to the conclusion (ensure the language of the variables is contained in the conclusions).

6 Provide children with different representations of evidence (in graph/table etc. form) and ask specific questions about that data.

7 Provide children with different sets of evidence for different investigations and allow them to discuss it and identify the patterns.

8 Use group talk methods to promote discussion of data rather than considering data individually.

9 Model the features of a good conclusion using the sequence for teaching writing (see Figure 4.4 below).

10 Provide children with opportunities to use their results further – for example, 'How many would you need to … ?'

11 Talk about the science behind the phenomena, not just at the beginning of the investigation but throughout. Give opportunities for the pupils to explore their evidence and the theory together.

12 Provide sets of evidence that refute an original question or prediction and allow children to form statements of what it might mean.

13 Provide the opportunity to look at data with errors in it and explore if the evidence can be trusted.

14 Provide writing frames such as the 'concluding' mat provided at the end of this chapter to help form causal statements and conclusions.

A good conclusion:

- starts by describing what the results show and if they could answer the question
- identifies any pattern in the results
- uses scientific terms
- attempts to explain the results
- makes a link between the variables (if relevant).

Figure 4.4 A good conclusion.

Questions to help develop analysing skills relating to different types of investigations

Can you answer your question for me?

Describe your results for me.

What do you think these results tell you?

What bit of evidence did you use to answer your question?

Was your prediction correct?

Did you expect that to happen?

Can you see any pattern in your results?

Can you spot any connection between … and … ?

Can you spot any surprises in the evidence?

So using your results if I … what would happen to … ?

Can you use all the evidence to answer the question?

Is there any evidence you cannot use to answer the question?

Was one bit of evidence better than another?

Could your evidence be used to answer another question?

There follows three contexts to explore and develop the skill of raising questions, predicting and planning, which directly relate to the new programme of study. These are:

Years 1 and 2 – Investigating seeds
Years 3 and 4 – Investigating rocks and soils
Years 5 and 6 – Investigating circulation.

Interpreting, analysing and concluding

Years 1 and 2: Investigating seeds

Working scientifically

Working at age-related expectations (Years 1 and 2)

Use observations and ideas to suggest answers to questions.

Non-statutory guidance: With guidance, the children should begin to notice patterns and relationships. They should ask people questions and use simple secondary sources to find answers.

Working above age-related expectations (Years 3+)

Use results to draw simple conclusions, make predictions for new values, suggest improvements and raise further questions.

Identify differences, similarities or changes related to simple scientific ideas and processes.

Use straightforward scientific evidence to answer questions or to support their findings.

Non-statutory guidance: With help, pupils should look for changes, patterns, similarities and differences in their data in order to draw simple conclusions and answer questions.

Year 1 and 2 context

Working at age-related expectations

Observe and describe how seeds and bulbs grow into mature plants.

Mathematics

Working at age-related expectations (Year 1)

Number
Count to and across 100, forwards and backwards, beginning with 0 or 1, or from any given number.

Count, read and write numbers to 100 in numerals; count in multiples of twos, fives and tens.

Given a number, identify one more and one less.

Identify and represent numbers using objects and pictorial representations including the number line, and use the language of: equal to, more than, less than (fewer), most, least.

Read and write numbers from 1 to 20 in numerals and words.

Measurement
Measure and begin to record the following: lengths and heights.

Compare, describe and solve practical problems for: lengths and heights (for example, long/short, longer/shorter, tall/short, double/half).

Teacher information

Seeds are embryonic plants (baby plants) contained in a protective outer coat. They usually contain an embryonic shoot (a plumule), an embryonic root (a radicle) and a food store to help them develop their first leaves.

A seed turns into a small plant by the process of *germination.* This involves the seed coat splitting and the plumule and radicle growing in length. In the first stages the seed uses the food store for its energy. Once the leaves have emerged and the roots are developed enough, the seed grows as any other plant and photosynthesises for its energy.

Shoots and roots grow rapidly to get what they need: sunlight and water. There is a misconception that seeds need a light source to germinate; they do not. They do, however, need water and an adequate temperature.

Some seeds are contained within layers of material rich in carbohydrates and fats. These are known as fruits and many things considered as 'seeds' are actually fruits.

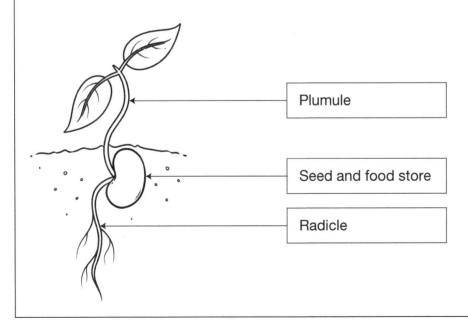

Launch pad

Give out the launch pad activity. Pose the question: 'Does **a** root grow faster than a shoot?' (This is adapted from an activity that can be found on the SAP's website: see Bibliography).

Run the investigation over a number of days (you can vary it from group to group by type of seed). Once the children have their outcomes, ask them to communicate to you what they have found out. The emphasis of this should not be in how they present what they have found out but on the quality of concluding statements they make and to what extent they make use of evidence.

Remember this is your base-line assessment and will provide you with information about their attainment in relation to ARE.

Ask the children to complete the first column of the self-assessment sheet.

Resources

Types of seed, e.g. bean, cress, radish, rapid-growing brassica

Petri dishes

Acetate sheets with grid or graph paper

Rulers

Water

Activity 1

Target group: Years 1 and 2 who are working at ARE.
Aim: To use observations and ideas to suggest answers to questions.

What to do

Look at a set of beans that has been growing in a variety of places. Pose the question: 'What do bean plants need to grow big and strong?'

Look at all the seeds with the children and explore with them what they are seeing and which one grew big and strong. Obtain the evidence (there is an opportunity to discuss with children what they will look for and/or measure – the things to guide them towards are length of stem, number of leaves, colour of leaves, length of roots).

Give out the basic concluding mat. Look at the central section and establish that we want to get an answer to our question. We start with what we wanted to find out, we then say if we have got an answer and say what the answer is.

Conclude the activity by using the central box to record the answer to the question and, if possible, extend by encouraging the use of one piece of evidence that they have noted. Use the questions below to try to elicit the answers.

Tips

- We are looking for children to make a judgement on which one looks the best to them. If children select their 'best one' – for example, the bean that has grown the most – and can tell you what conditions it has grown under then this is evidence of ARE at Years 1 and 2.
- At this stage the children will look for the tallest plant but allow for other interpretations, particularly if the bean plant is tall or stringy and pale green. They might also observe the lengths of the roots.
- Be aware of evidence of causality that indicates above ARE, for example if they start using the connective 'because' in relation to questions you might ask.
- If children want to do some measurement to prove their ideas this is also an indication that they are working above ARE.
- Seeds take time to grow. Build this timing into your planning.

Key questions to develop the skill

- Which one looks big and strong?
- What does it look like? How big is it?
- What did we do to the seed?
- Did the seed grow well if ...?

Key vocabulary

Shoot, stem, leaf, root, big, tall, long

Resources

Pre-grown plants from a variety of conditions such as dark, light, cold, warmth, watered, not watered

Activity 2

Target group: Years 1 and 2 working above ARE.
Aim: To use evidence to make conclusions.

What to do

The question is the same as in Activity 1, but the focus is using the evidence and thus an element of pattern seeking. Measure or provide the children with measurements of stem length, root length, number of leaves, and appearance of the leaves from an investigation with the same question as in the previous activity. Ensure the evidence is in a form that they can work with. Make sure the evidence is very clear and does not leave any room for ambiguity. Use the basic concluding mats to complete the sections on 'My evidence' and if they spot a pattern look at the 'My pattern' section. Model answering the question and completing the 'because' section using the evidence.

Tips

- Be careful of the difference between *conditions for germination* and *conditions for growth* – they are different. In this investigation we are looking at conditions for growth.
- To make this more kinaesthetic, provide the children with pre-grown plants as in the previous activity.
- Agree with the children the question and the evidence you will look for in relation to the question before you complete the investigation. For example, 'What is big and strong? What are we looking for?'
- Unless you want to widen the focus, be sure the emphasis does not turn into making measurements.
- If children are struggling with the measurements, have them printed out beforehand and attached to each plant so they can see the concrete bigger stem with the bigger number.
- Try sequencing the plants in order of size of stem to come up with the best plant.
- This task is okay to complete as a group activity.
- If the children can use the word 'conclusion' you can introduce it to them.

Key questions to develop the skill

- How do we know if it has grown well?
- Which plant has the longest stem?
- Which plant has the longest root?
- Which plant has the most leaves?
- Which plant looks the best?
- Did the seed need light?
- Did the seed need water?
- Did the seed need warmth?

Key vocabulary

Shoot, stem, leaf, root, big, tall, long, evidence, results, pattern, conclusion

Resources

Tables of data on measurements of stem length, root length, number of leaves from a seed grown under a variety of conditions, *or*

Seeds that have been growing under different conditions – for example cold, warm, dark, light, lots of water, no water

Rulers in mm, cm, m

The final activity

For the final activity review the original launch pad task. Ask the children to tell you if they have changed their minds and amend, annotate their original work or note down any new concluding statements that they have made.

Ask the children to complete the second column of the self-assessment sheet.

Interpreting, analysing and concluding

Years 3 and 4: Investigating rocks and soils

Working scientifically

Working towards age-related expectations (Years 1 and 2)

Use observations and ideas to suggest answers to questions.

Non-statutory guidance: With guidance, the children should begin to notice patterns and relationships. They should ask people questions and use simple secondary sources to find answers.

Working at age-related expectations (Years 3 and 4)

Use results to draw simple conclusions, make predictions for new values, suggest improvements and raise further questions.

Identify differences, similarities or changes related to simple scientific ideas and processes.

Use straightforward scientific evidence to answer questions or to support their findings.

Non-statutory guidance: With help, pupils should look for changes, patterns, similarities and differences in their data in order to draw simple conclusions and answer questions.

Working above age-related expectations (Years 5 and 6)

Report and present findings from enquiries, including conclusions, causal relationships and explanations of, and degree of trust in, results in oral and written forms such as displays and other presentations.

Identify scientific evidence that has been used to support or refute ideas or arguments.

Non-statutory guidance: Look for different causal relationships in their data and identify evidence that refutes or supports their ideas.

Years 3 and 4 context

Working at age-related expectations

Recognise that soils are made from rocks and organic matter.

Compare and group together different kinds of rocks on the basis of their appearance and simple physical properties.

Mathematics

Working at age-related expectations (Year 3)

Number
Count from 0 in multiples of 4, 8, 50 and 100.

Find 10 or 100 more or less than a given number.

Recognise the place value of each digit in a three-digit number (hundreds, tens, and ones).

Compare and order numbers up to 1000.

Identify, represent and estimate numbers using different representations.

Read and write numbers up to 1000 in numerals and in words.

Solve number problems and practical problems involving these ideas.

Measurement
Measure, compare, add and subtract: lengths (m/cm/mm); mass (kg/g); volume/capacity (l/ml).

Teacher information

There are three types of rock, which are formed in different ways.

1 **Igneous rock** was once liquid rock (magma). It can be made inside the Earth when the magma cools or on the surface when lava cools. An example of an igneous rock made inside the Earth is granite. An example of an igneous rock formed on the surface is basalt or pumice.
2 **Sedimentary rock** is usually the softest kind and is made from particles of sand, clay, animal or plant remains. These are compressed and eventually form rock. Examples of sedimentary rocks are chalk, limestone, sandstone, mudstone, shale, coal. You find fossils in sedimentary rock.
3 **Metamorphic rock** is formed when rock under the surface is compressed by forces inside the Earth. The compressed rock also experiences very high temperatures. This forms rocks like marble and slate.

Soils are made up of two main components: the initial rocks that the soil was formed from and organic matter from dead and decaying plants and animals.

Soils absorb water and retain it, or they allow water to pass freely through it (this is important for the plants that can grow in the soil). The ability to retain water is related to the particle sizes within the soil and how densely packed they are. If a soil consists of very small, densely packed particles (such as a clay soil) then it will retain the water. If a soil's particles are large and loosely packed (such as in sandy soil) the water will tend to flow faster through it.

Launch pad

Give out the launch pad activity. Ask the question: 'Which is the hardest rock?'

Give the children a basic method for carrying out this investigation (remember the emphasis is on concluding, therefore it is okay for this not to be an open-ended investigation). There are two methods you can try: the scratch test (to see how easy it is scratched) and shaking a sample of rock in a dry, sealed plastic bottle to see how much is broken off (measured by the mass before and after). Run the investigation and eavesdrop and take note of what the children are doing. Ask them to communicate to you what they have found out.

The emphasis of this should not be in how they present what they have found out but on the concluding statements they make. Therefore you can provide them with methods and templates to record/present their results. Alternatively, you can provide them with sets of data for them to look at and tell you what they think they mean.

Remember this is your base-line assessment and will provide you with information about the children's attainment in relation to ARE.

Ask the children to complete the first column of the self-assessment sheet.

Resources

Rock samples

Iron nail, fingernail (to scratch with)

Tray to collect bits

Safety goggles

Empty dry plastic bottles with lids

Scales (digital)

Mohs hardness scale

Activity 1

Target group: Years 3 and 4 who are working towards ARE.

Aim: To use observations and ideas to suggest answers to questions.

What to do

Pose the question. The options are: 'Which soil does water run through fastest?' or 'Which soil absorbs the most water?' Carry out the investigation (or use the support data sheet provided). Look at all the funnels and explore with the children what they are seeing/observing.

Give out the basic concluding mat. Look at the sections and establish that we want to get an answer for our question. We start with what we wanted to find out, we then say if we have got an answer and say what the answer is. Conclude the activity by using the central box to try to record their answer to the question and if possible extend by encouraging the use of one piece of evidence that they have noted.

Tips

- At this stage the children will make general statements and not really use the numerical evidence, just their observations. We are looking for children to make a judgement on which one either lets the water through fastest or retains the most water.
- Be aware of evidence of causality that indicates above ARE – for example, if they start using the connective 'because' in relation to questions you might ask.
- If children want to do some measurement to prove their ideas this is also an indication that they are working above ARE.

Key questions to develop the skill

- How do you know it soaked up most of the water? What piece of evidence could you use?
- How do you know it went through faster? What piece of evidence could you use?

Key vocabulary

Soil, water, funnel, time, soak, absorb, dense, permeability, drain

Resources

Samples of soil with various compositions of sand, clay, humus

Measuring cylinders

Funnels with filter paper

Stopwatches

Plastic beakers

Activity 2

Target group: Years 3 and 4 who are working at ARE.
Aim: To use evidence to make conclusions.

What to do

Pose the question. The options are: 'Which soil does water run through fastest?' or 'Which soil absorbs the most water?' The question is the same, but the focus is using the evidence and thus an element of pattern-seeking.

Carry out the investigation (or use the Investigating soil support sheet provided). Look at the amount of water poured into the soil/amount of water that passed through the soil/time taken for water to pass through the soil into a measuring cylinder. Ensure the evidence is in a form that the children can work with. Make sure the evidence is very clear and does not leave any room for ambiguity.

Use the basic concluding mats to complete the section on 'My evidence' and if they spot a pattern look at the 'My pattern' section. Model answering the question and completing the 'Because' section using the evidence.

Tips

- Agree with the children the question and the evidence you will look for in relation to the question, for example time or volume.
- Unless you want to widen the focus, be sure the emphasis does not turn into making measurements.
- If children are struggling with the measurements, have them printed out beforehand and attached to the funnel so they can see the concrete number.
- Try sequencing the soils in order of how much water passed through/how fast it passed through.
- This task is suitable to complete as a group activity.

Key questions to develop the skill

- Can you put the soils in order?
- Which one let through the most water?
- What evidence are we looking for here?
- What are we looking for when we do this investigation?

Key vocabulary

Soil, water, funnel, time, soak, absorb, dense, permeability, drain, evidence, results, pattern, conclusion

Resources

Samples of soil with various compositions of sand/clay/humus

Measuring cylinders

Funnels with filter paper

Stopwatches

Plastic beakers

Tables of data: Amount of water poured into the soil/Amount of water that passed through the soil/Time taken for water to pass through the soil

Activity 3

Target group: Years 3 and 4 who are working above ARE.

Aim: To report and present findings from enquiries, including conclusions, causal relationships and explanations of, and discuss the degree of trust in the evidence.

To identify scientific evidence that has been used to support or refute ideas or arguments.

What to do

Provide the children with the questions in the previous investigations and sample sets of data. Provide relevant data that can answer the questions using the principles of causality or use the support data sheet provided.

Now follow the sequence for teaching writing; provide the children with the three conclusions based upon the data from the investigating soils support sheet. Ask them to discuss the conclusions and agree on which one is the best. Now, using the children's input, come up with a list of rules for making a good conclusion. Refer to the advanced planning mat to model how we make concluding statements.

Take the other question and draft a conclusion together with the children using the rules. Use the advanced concluding mat to formulate the sentences, explaining at each point why we use this language.

Tip

● This task is suitable to complete as a group activity.

Key questions to develop the skill

● Which evidence could you use to answer this question and why?
● Why couldn't you use this piece of evidence?
● What would you need to do to this investigation to trust the data more?

Key vocabulary

Soil, water, funnel, time, soak, absorb, dense, permeability, drain, evidence, results, conclusions, patterns, trust, accuracy, precision

Resources

Samples of soil with various compositions of sand/clay/humus

Measuring cylinders

Funnels with filter paper

Stopwatches

Plastic beakers

Tables of data: Amount of water poured into the soil/Amount of water that passed through the soil/Time taken for water to pass through the soil

The final activity

For the final activity you will repeat/review the results from the original launch pad investigation. The emphasis of this should not be in how the children present what they have found out but on the quality of the concluding statements they make. You will be using this to judge the progress made in the skill area.

Ask the children to complete the second column of the self-assessment sheet.

Interpreting, analysing and concluding

Years 5 and 6: Investigating circulation

Working scientifically

Working towards age-related expectations (Years 5 and 6)

Use results to draw simple conclusions, make predictions for new values, suggest improvements and raise further questions.

Identify differences, similarities or changes related to simple scientific ideas and processes.

Use straightforward scientific evidence to answer questions or to support their findings.

Non-statutory guidance: With help, pupils should look for changes, patterns, similarities and differences in their data in order to draw simple conclusions and answer questions.

Working at age-related expectations (Years 5 and 6)

Report and present findings from enquiries, including conclusions, causal relationships and explanations of, and degree of trust in, results in oral and written forms such as displays and other presentations.

Identify scientific evidence that has been used to support or refute ideas or arguments.

Non-statutory guidance: Look for different causal relationships in their data and identify evidence that refutes or supports their ideas.

Year 5 and 6 context

Working at age-related expectations

Identify and name the main parts of the human circulatory system, and describe the functions of the heart, blood vessels and blood.

Describe the ways in which nutrients and water are transported within animals, including humans.

Mathematics

Working at age-related expectations (Year 5)

Number
Read, write, order and compare numbers to at least 1,000,000 and determine the value of each digit.

Count forwards or backwards in steps of powers of 10 for any given number up to 1,000,000.

Measurement
Convert between different units of metric measure (for example, kilometre and metre; centimetre and metre; centimetre and millimetre; gram and kilogram; litre and millilitre).

Teacher information

Blood is the main medium for transport and exchange of substances necessary for life. It also has an important role to play in the body's defence system. Humans (like other but not all animals) have a double circulatory system. That means the blood is pumped around the body in two different directions. One route is for gaseous exchange and the other route is for delivery and exchange of substances necessary for life.

The heart is a pump that is made of muscle called 'cardiac muscle'. It is made up of four chambers. The two chambers at the top of the heart are called the atria (one is an atrium). The atria are the chambers that fill with the blood returning to the heart from the body and lungs. The heart has a left atrium and a right atrium. The two chambers on the bottom are called the ventricles. The heart has a left ventricle and a right ventricle. Their job is to pump the blood to the body and lungs. The atria and ventricles work to circulate the blood – the atria fill with blood and then pass it into the ventricles. The ventricles then pump blood out of the heart at a high pressure. While the ventricles are squeezing, the atria refill and get ready for the next contraction.

Blood is circulated in tubes called arteries, veins and capillaries. The arteries are the largest and thickest vessels and carry blood at higher pressure. The veins are less muscular and carry blood at lower pressure. (There is a common misconception that all arteries carry blood away from the heart, but this is not the case.)

Capillaries are very small and have very thin walls. Their job is to facilitate exchange of substances, such as gases and nutrients, across their surface.

Launch pad

Give out the launch pad activity. Introduce the context that the children are exploring: what happens to heart and breathing rate as you exercise. Pose the question: 'Who is the fittest in the class?' Discuss what we mean by 'fitness'. If possible, take predictions – it is not necessary to over-emphasise this as you are teaching a different skill.

Give out a basic method for carrying out this investigation (remember the emphasis is on concluding therefore it is okay for this not to be an open-ended investigation). Run the investigation and eavesdrop and take note on what the children are doing. Ask them to present what they have found out. The emphasis of this should not be in how they present what they have found out but on the concluding statements they make. Therefore you can provide them with methods and templates for them to record/present their results. If you do not wish to carry out this investigation, then you can provide the children with the sets of data to use.

Remember this is your base-line assessment and will provide you with information about the children's attainment in relation to ARE.

Ask the children to complete the first column of the self-assessment sheet.

Activity 1

Target group: Years 5 and 6 who are working towards ARE.
Aim: To use evidence to make conclusions.

What to do

Give an original question such as 'Who has the fastest pulse rate after exercise, boys or girls?' Model for the children and then ask them to take their pulse rate and record it in the table provided. Try to collate all the class results. Also record all the heights of the children (a model set of data is provided in the support sheets section).

Use the basic concluding mats to complete the sections on the question and 'My evidence' and 'My patterns' that can be used to make 'The answer to my question is...' Discuss with the children what their answer will be and what evidence they have based this on. Discuss with the children the fact that the height information could not be used to answer this question unless we noticed a new pattern such as boys were taller than girls or vice versa.

Model for the children how we would make a conclusion using the concluding phrases and words on the advanced concluding mat.

Tips

- Agree with the children the question and the evidence you will look for in relation to the question, for example beats per minute and number of girls or boys.
- Unless you want to widen the focus, be sure the emphasis (and bulk of time) does not turn into taking measurements (this is the means to collect the evidence).
- If children are struggling with the measurements, model the process and then let them do it independently. Do not correct any obvious mistakes but take note of them.
- Try presenting the evidence in another way.
- Introduce different types of evidence to explore if they are relevant or not.
- Try kinaesthetically sequencing the class in order of pulse rate to present the evidence in a more visual way.

Key questions to develop the skill

- Is there a pattern?
- Do all the girls have a ... pulse rate? Do all the boys have a ... pulse rate?
- What evidence are we looking for here? What are we looking for when we do this investigation?
- What do you notice?

Key vocabulary

Circulation, pulse, breath, evidence, fitness, results, conclusions, patterns

Resources

Stopwatches/pulse meters if available

Activity 2

Target group: Years 5 and 6 who are working at ARE.

Aim: To report and present findings from enquiries, including conclusions, causal relationships and explanations of, and degree of trust.

What to do

Provide the children with the question in the previous investigations or a similar one and sample sets of data. Provide relevant data that can answer the questions using the principles of causality (a model set of data is provided in the support sheets section). Include irrelevant data and data that have no clear pattern to them so cannot be used. If possible, include data where there is an issue relating to accuracy or precision.

Now follow the sequence for teaching writing: provide the children with three conclusions based upon the data answering one question (see Investigating circulation support sheet). Ask them to discuss the conclusions and agree on which one is the best. Now, using the children's input, come up with a list of rules for making a good conclusion. Refer to the advanced planning mat to model how we make concluding statements. Take the other question and draft a conclusion together with the children, using the rules. Use the advanced concluding mat to formulate the sentences, explaining at each point why we use this language.

Tips

- This task is suitable to complete as a group activity.
- Use the 'concluding mat' to record key learning points and vocabulary.

Key questions to develop the skill

- Which evidence could you use to answer this question and why?
- Why couldn't you use this piece of evidence?
- What would you need to do to this investigation to trust the data more?

Key vocabulary

Resting, pulse, circulation, data, results, evidence, trust, accuracy, precision, patterns, conclusions

Resources

Stopwatches/pulse meters if available

Sample sets of data

The final activity

For the final activity you will repeat/review their original launch pad investigation. Ask the children to look at their data again and now say what they have found out/improve upon it. The emphasis of this should not be in how they present what they have found out but on the quality of the concluding statements they make. You will be using this to judge the progress made in the skill area.

Ask the children to complete the second column of the self-assessment sheet.

5   Reflecting and evaluating

The skill of evaluation in 'Working scientifically' requires children to develop the ability to reflect on and make judgements on the process and outcomes of an investigation against a definite set of criteria which may be related to what they have done or how they have done something, and also the relevance of what they have found out in relation to answering the question. It is one of the cognitive domains located towards the pinnacle of Bloom's taxonomy: Remember—Comprehend—Understand—Apply—Analyse—Evaluate.

For these reasons evaluation is a very challenging set of skills for children (and adults alike) and unless they have been taught how to evaluate, the most one can hope for is a superficial comment or two about how easy or difficult they found the investigation or if they worked well or not. In my experience difficulties in this area are persistent and I have taught A-level students with limited evaluation skills. However, if handled carefully and with an eye on how the skills can be developed we can help children progress in this area.

This development is reflected in the ARE of the National Curriculum in England: Science programmes of study (see Figure 5.1). Looking at this in another way and in a bit more detail, we can gain a sense of what skills might be inherent in these steps yet are not explicitly mentioned, those that are earlier in the development and later in the development (see Figure 5.2). You will see that this skill relies on the child understanding both the physical process of an investigation (planning and carrying out) and the nature of the evidence derived from the investigation and it is because it is intimately linked with analysis of evidence that it is often not explicitly taught, this then leads to confusion and ultimately less developed evaluation skills.

Lower primary Years 1 and 2	Ask simple questions and recognise they can be answered in different ways. Guidance (*non-statutory*): They should experience different types of scientific enquiries, including practical activities, and begin to recognise ways in which they might answer scientific questions.
Lower Key Stage 2 Years 3 and 4	Use results to draw simple conclusions, make predictions for new values, suggest improvements and raise further questions. Guidance (*non-statutory*): With support, they should identify new questions arising from the data, making predictions for new values within or beyond the data they have collected and finding ways of improving what they have already done.
Upper Key Stage 2 Years 5 and 6	Report and present findings from enquiries, including conclusions, causal relationships and explanations of **and degree of trust in results, in oral and written forms such as displays and other presentations**. Identify scientific evidence that has been used to support or refute ideas or arguments. Use test results to make predictions to set up further comparative and fair tests. Guidance (*non-statutory*): They should use their results to identify when further tests and observations might be needed; recognise which secondary sources will be most useful to research their ideas and begin to separate opinion from fact.

Figure 5.1 Progress in ARE in the skill area of reflecting and evaluating evidence (National Curriculum in England: Science programmes of study 2015).

Basic skills	Advanced skills
Deciding if their investigation answered the question or not	Deciding to what extent their investigation answered the question
Exploring different ways to answer the same question	Identifying the most effective way to answer the question after trying alternatives
Evaluation uses non-scientific vocabulary to express evaluative statements	Evaluation uses scientific language and if possible concepts of causality, accuracy and precision
Limited suggestions for technical improvement involving practical equipment/ methodology or vague statements such as 'it was easy', 'work harder' and 'don't mess around'	Evaluation reflects both on methodology and how this might affect the confidence in or degree of trust in the evidence
Limited appreciation of the use of evidence to simple contextual inquiries	Identify scientific evidence that has been used to support or refute more abstract ideas or arguments
Accepts that their prediction was right or wrong	Using what they have found out to amend and make further predictions
Evaluation focused on what went wrong and identifying the data that cannot be used	Evaluation contains elements of hypothesising why the data cannot be used

Figure 5.2 A simple model of progress in the skills of reflection and evaluation.

Barriers to progress

Misconceptions in context. In the case of evaluation, a persistent misconception in the context (knowledge and understanding) can prevent the child from accepting that their prediction could have been wrong or the child will see the evidence only through their original idea and cannot accept the challenge to their idea.

Using absolute statements. Even though we try to teach the children that there is no right or wrong in an investigation, children still measure their success against 'getting it right'. This can lead to limited evaluations, especially when trying to discuss degrees of trust. Also they may not like to admit it if they made errors, so if you ask a probing question – 'Did you measure this accurately?' – the response may well be 'yes'.

Judgements. The above can prompt a feeling of being judged if their conclusions are questioned. This, in turn, can trigger negative behaviour responses within the enquiry process.

Language. Children do not always have the vocabulary to communicate limitations in evidence. This is particularly important when there are issues with reliability or precision and can be very frustrating for children and adults alike! It can be especially problematic if the teacher does not have it clear in their own mind what these terms mean (see previous discussion in Chapter 3).

Planning of the tasks. The children may also not understand the nature of the language and features of a good evaluation (see Figure 5.3) and this has a direct impact on teaching, especially when teaching this skill to upper primary age children. The tasks and types of investigation set by the teacher may not be conducive to more complex and abstract evaluations. First, if the task is one that will only elicit subjective and qualitative evidence it is more difficult to apply the idea of precision and accuracy in relation to the evidence and therefore children will not develop in this area. It is not possible to comment on fairness if the investigation is not originally a comparative or fair test. Second, the teacher could, with the best intentions, supply the pupils with a question that needs to be explored. Although this is valid and can be used, this takes away the huge potential for autonomy and creativity to come up with new questions and directions for the investigation. Another issue might arise if the children are given the equipment and a set of instructions on how to use it. Again, this is valid but taking away the possibility of new and novel ways to use the equipment means the evaluation might be limited to how well the child used the equipment not on *why* they chose to use that piece of equipment in that particular way.

Questioning and eliciting ideas. The questions asked by the teacher can limit the response by the child (closed versus open-ended questions). For example, 'Can you trust your results?' as opposed to 'To what extent can you trust your results?' Often simple, closed questions require subsequent more open questions to encourage deeper learning and reflection on the nature of the evidence.

Accessing the planning process. Evaluation and reflection skills are also intimately linked with all the other 'Working scientifically' skills as the children need to access and understand the whole planning process to be able to make a value judgement about it and the evidence they have gathered. If they have not developed their skills in the other areas, high level evaluations may not be possible.

Suggestions for the teacher

1   Design beforehand the types of questions you wish to ask and make them directly relevant to the investigation.
2   Give an exemplar set of results that requires the children to evaluate, ensuring there is an appropriate mix of results.
3   Use group work to allow children to talk to each other about the results and the methods used.
4   Create a separate teaching sequence to develop the idea of accuracy and precision by setting up a circus of measuring stations where you know the true value of the measurement and then ask the children to measure and record in a pre-prepared table the measurements they take. Review the range of measurements the children took.
5   Provide and model investigative processes to allow children to judge if the methods are appropriate for the question.
6   Play 'spot the error'. Carry out investigations in front of the children and include deliberate 'mistakes' or vague statements or measurements and ask them to spot the mistake. (A version of this is a game called 'Blooper' that can be found in *Science Enquiry Games* by Goldsworthy and Ponchaud, 2007.)
7   Provide writing frames, such as the evaluating mats in this guide, in order to help the children frame their evaluative statements.
8   Provide some contextual examples of data that children can discuss and judge if it has been used to support an argument.
9   Use questioning (see above) to probe deeper into the children's reflective statements to explore their understanding of accuracy, precision and degrees of trust in data.

10 'Think out loud' – get the children to articulate their thought processes as they are conducting the investigation. Give the children questions or a framework to help them do this.

11 Invite children to teach another child in the class the way to do something and then ask the one being taught to give feedback on how to make it better.

12 Organise children into teams and give them an investigation with obvious errors in it. Ask them to work as a team to improve the investigation to get the best possible outcomes and then complete the investigation to see if they answered the question.

Key questions to ask in reflecting and evaluation

What was the question you wanted to answer?

Did you find an answer to your question?

How did you decide to do it?

What could you have done differently to answer the question?

What did your results show?

Based on what you found out, what do you think would happen if…?

What was the hardest part to do?

How difficult was it to collect your evidence?

Did all your equipment work okay?

Did you make any mistakes when you were using the equipment?

Did you make any mistakes when you were measuring? What could you do to correct those mistakes?

What are the chances that someone doing exactly what you did would get the same results?

Did you choose the best way to present your results?

Could you think of a clearer way to present your results?

Are there any results that don't seem to fit your ideas/predictions? Can you explain why they don't fit?

What did that scientist use to back up their ideas?

How much could you trust your results? Why can't you trust them? Why do you trust them?

What alternative conclusions can you draw from your results?

If you did this again, what would you change to make it better?

How would you get more accurate results?

How would you get more precise results?

Can you think of another question you could answer with this method?

If you did this investigation again what prediction could you make?

Do you agree with what was done …?

How would you prove …? How would you disprove …?

How important was …?

Would it be better if …?

What would you recommend …?

How would you rate the …?

There follows three contexts to explore and develop the skill of raising questions, predicting and planning which directly relate to the new programme of study. These are:

Years 1 and 2 – Investigating habitats

Years 3 and 4 – Investigating teeth

Years 5 and 6 – Investigating insulation.

A good evaluation:

- states if the question could be answered or not
- suggest ways to improve the experiment (ways of working, equipment etc.)
- discusses if there are enough results to spot a pattern
- discusses whether, if the measurements were repeated, there was a wide variation or they were similar
- discusses accuracy by commenting on how accurate the measuring instruments are or how accurate are the observations
- identifies possible errors
- states how much they trust their evidence because of all the above
- maybe discusses what else could they find out using these results
- maybe states what else would they like to know.

Figure 5.3 Teacher information.

Reflecting and evaluating

Years 1 and 2: Investigating habitats

Working scientifically

Working at age-related expectations

Ask simple questions and recognise they can be answered in different ways.

Guidance *(non-statutory)*: The children should experience different types of scientific enquiries, including practical activities, and begin to recognise ways in which they might answer scientific questions.

Working above age-related expectations

Use results to draw simple conclusions, make predictions for new values, suggest improvements and raise further questions.

Guidance *(non-statutory)*: With support, they should identify new questions arising from the data, making predictions for new values within or beyond the data they have collected and finding ways of improving what they have already done.

Knowledge and understanding

Working at age-related expectations

Identify that most living things live in habitats to which they are suited and describe how different habitats provide for the basic needs of different kinds of animals and plants, and how they depend on each other.

Identify and name a variety of plants and animals in their habitats, including microhabitats.

Mathematics

Working at age-related expectations (Year 1)

Number

Count to and across 100, forwards and backwards, beginning with 0 or 1, or from any given number.

Count, read and write numbers to 100 in numerals; count in multiples of twos, fives and tens.

Given a number, identify one more and one less.

Identify and represent numbers using objects and pictorial representations including the number line, and use the language of: equal to, more than, less than (fewer), most, least.

Read and write numbers from 1 to 20 in numerals and words.

Measurement

Measure and begin to record the following: lengths and heights.

Compare, describe and solve practical problems for: lengths and heights (for example, long/short, longer/shorter, tall/short, double/half).

Teacher information

A habitat is the place where an organism lives. It provides the basics for life. A habitat is made up of physical (abiotic) factors such as soil, moisture, temperature, and availability of light as well as biotic factors such as the availability of food, predators and mates.

A woodlouse is a common arthropod. It is an animal but it is NOT an insect although it is often called a bug. Its ideal habitat is a moist, dark area. Woodlice are often studied in schools because their behaviour is clear. We can see what habitats they prefer by using a piece of equipment called a 'choice chamber'. The choices on offer to the woodlice tend to be light and dry, light and damp, dark and dry, and dark and damp. The woodlice are left in these conditions for a while and then counted. You should find that the majority of woodlice are found in the damp and dark conditions.

Launch pad

Provide the children with the launch pad activity. Both the children (Lucy and George) in the activity have ideas of where to find them and suggest things they can do. Encourage the children to reflect on what Lucy and George are suggesting and which one they think will work best. Encourage them to think of some other ways to answer the question.

Remember this is your base-line assessment so do not intervene at this point. If the children are struggling to suggest ways to find out then they can put 'I do not know' or a '?'.

Ask the children to complete the first column of the self-assessment sheet.

Activity 1

Target group: Years 1 and 2 working at ARE.
Aim: To develop the skill of asking simple questions and to recognise that they can be answered in different ways.

What to do

Introduce the context that they are exploring woodlice. Use suitable materials to introduce the woodlice and emphasise that these are living things and should be treated with respect (if you are squeamish and bug phobic this may not be for you).

Look at the woodlice and ask the children what they would like to know about them.

Encourage the children to formulate a question or two about the woodlice. Use the basic evaluation mat to help formulate the questions. Model one question formulation about the woodlice and then highlight the main question stems and connectives in the main body of the question. Allow children to brainstorm for a while and draw or write their responses (some might use oral explanations). Display responses on a learning wall.

The final part consists of providing stimuli for different ways to answer the question. Have around the room the means to answer 'generally' the questions and then allow the children to try to find out the answer to their question. Finish the session by evaluating how many of them found the answer to their question and review a list of the ways they used.

Key questions to develop the skill

- What question did we want to answer?
- Who could answer the question?
- Who found out where woodlice like to live?
- Did you find out your answer?
- What do you think you needed to do to find your answer?
- I wonder … Do you think?
- What would you like to know more about? What do you want to find out?
- How could you do that? What do you need to do?

Key vocabulary

Question stems: what, when, why, where, how

Questions, investigate, ideas, answer

Resources

A book corner filled with books on invertebrates

A computer open with information about invertebrates

Observing equipment

Choice chambers

Brushes to handle the woodlice

Activity 2

Target group: Years 1 and 2 who are working above ARE.
Aim: To develop the skill of suggesting improvements to investigations.

What to do

Provide children with a specific question to answer, such as 'Do woodlice like to live in damp places?', 'Where do woodlice like to live?', 'Do woodlice prefer dark places?' Ask them to answer the question before they start the investigation (a basic prediction). Provide a basic investigation method (remember the emphasis is not on planning or presenting results). Once the results have been gathered, explore what they mean.

Use the basic evaluation mat to complete the relevant sections. Use questions to explore if the question was answered, what went well (WWW) and even better if (EBI). The aim is to get the children to reflect on the methodology used. Use the word and phrase bank to formulate sentences.

Tips

- If children are squeamish about handling woodlice do not force them to but model good practice and show how to manipulate/pick them up with a brush and then encourage them to have a go at moving the woodlice.
- Use this as a chance to reinforce previous work on differences between animals i.e. how is a woodlouse different to a fly.
- Carry this out as a group activity, encouraging talk in the investigations.

Key questions to develop the skill

- What did you do?
- Did it work?
- How difficult was it?

- What did your results mean?
- Did the woodlice do what you thought they would do?
- Did you answer the question?
- Could you think of another way to answer the question?
- Which way do you think is best?
- Did you make any mistakes?
- Was any bit really hard to do?
- Could you think of a better way of doing it?

Key vocabulary

- Question, investigation, ideas, answers, evaluation, why?, improvement, problem

Resources

- A book corner filled with books on invertebrates
- A computer open with information about invertebrates
- Observing equipment
- Choice chambers and woodlice, paper, leaf material, soil, sand, lamps
- Brushes to handle the woodlice

The final activity

Explore the launch pad activity again. Ask the children to add any more ideas that they have had.

Give out the self-assessment sheet and ask children to complete the second column.

Reflecting and evaluating

Years 3 and 4: Investigating teeth

Working scientifically

Working towards age-related expectations

Ask simple questions and recognise they can be answered in different ways.

Guidance *(non-statutory)*: The children should experience different types of scientific enquiries, including practical activities, and begin to recognise ways in which they might answer scientific questions.

Working at age-related expectations

Use results to draw simple conclusions, make predictions for new values, suggest improvements and raise further questions.

Guidance *(non-statutory)*: With support, they should identify new questions arising from the data, making predictions for new values within or beyond the data they have collected, and finding ways of improving what they have already done.

Working above age-related expectations

Report and present findings from enquiries, including conclusions, causal relationships and explanations of and degree of trust in results, in oral and written forms such as displays and other presentations.

Identify scientific evidence that has been used to support or refute ideas or arguments.

Use test results to make predictions to set up further comparative and fair tests.

Guidance *(non-statutory)*: They should use their results to identify when further tests and observations might be needed, recognise which secondary sources will be most useful to research their ideas and begin to separate opinion from fact.

Knowledge and understanding

Working at age-related expectations

Describe the simple functions of the basic parts of the digestive system in humans.

Identify the different types of teeth in humans and their simple function.

Mathematics

Working at age-related expectations (Year 3)

Number
Count from 0 in multiples of 4, 8, 50 and 100; find 10 or 100 more or less than a given number.

Recognise the place value of each digit in a three-digit number (hundreds, tens, ones).

Compare and order numbers up to 1000.

Identify, represent and estimate numbers using different representations.

Read and write numbers up to 1000 in numerals and in words.

Solve number problems and practical problems involving these ideas.

Measurement
Measure, compare, add and subtract: lengths (m/cm/mm); mass (kg/g); volume/capacity (l/ml).

Teacher information

Teeth play an important part in digestion. They cut, tear and grind food. This is known as mechanical digestion. Teeth are made of a core containing the nerves and blood vessels called 'pulp'; the next layer is called 'dentine'; and then a hard, outer layer is called enamel.

Enamel can be worn away by general wear and tear, but also by acidic materials. This acid erosion is called 'tooth decay'. Over a period of time the acid in foods and drinks react with the minerals in the enamel and it gradually erodes. Fizzy drinks are one of the principal causes of tooth decay as they contain high levels of sugar and carbonic acid.

Another cause of tooth decay is plaque. Plaque is made up of bacteria that feed on the sugar found in what we eat and drink. When foods containing sugars are eaten, the bacteria in plaque break down the sugars and acid is produced. This acid then erodes the surface of the enamel under the plaque, causing the decay.

Launch pad

PRIOR WARNING: The day before, put eggshell in fizzy water, orange juice and water.

Provide the children with the launch pad activity and the data from an investigation (you can use the data in the support sheets section).

Ask the following questions:

● What is Susie trying to find out?
● Can you think of some other questions she could answer with this investigation?
● Look at what she did. Would you do anything differently?
● Can you think of any ways to improve her investigation?

Get children to record their responses on the launch pad sheet. Remember this is your base-line assessment so do not intervene at this point. If the children are struggling to suggest ways to find out, they can put 'I don't know' or a '?'.

Ask the children to complete the first column of the self-assessment sheet.

Activity 1

Target group: Years 3 and 4 who are working towards ARE.
Aim: To develop the skill of asking simple questions and recognise that they can be answered in different ways.

What to do

You are going to try Susie's investigation. Introduce the context that they are exploring tooth decay. About two days before, put a whole egg in a jar of clear vinegar, show the children the egg, and explain that the shell is similar to the coating on their teeth, only their tooth enamel is much thicker. Observe it over a few days: the shell will dissolve, leaving the inner skin of the egg. Show the children a range of equipment that Susie could have used to investigate this concept and ask them to think of some questions that they would like the answers to. Around the room provide the means to answer 'generally' the questions and then invite the children to try to find out the answer to their question. Finish the session by evaluating how many of them found the answer to their question and review a list of the ways they used.

Use the basic evaluation mat to record if they could answer their question and the ways they answered it. If possible, start thinking by using the WWW and EBI sections about ways to improve the investigation and record those.

Tips

- Introduce the model of eggshell = teeth before this session. Some children find models difficult to understand.
- Allow time for exploration.
- You could try peer assessment of the children's questions using a set of criteria such as 'Is it an interesting question?'
- Develop a key vocabulary bank to assist in the formulation of questions and techniques.
- Laminate the question stems so that if a child wants to ask a question they can pick up the question stem, hold it up and orally ask their question.
- Allow time for the children to talk and develop a fixed number of questions or as many as they can think of in a fixed period of time.
- Ask the children to list the equipment they would need to answer their question.

Key questions to develop the skill

- I wonder … Do you think?
- What would you like to know more about? What do you want to find out?
- How could you do that? What do you need to do? Where would you find that out?
- Did you find out your answer? What do you think you needed to do to find your answer?
- Could you think of a different way to answer the question?

Key vocabulary

Question stems: what, when, why, where, how

Questions, investigate, ideas, answer

Resources

A book corner filled with books on teeth

A computer open with information about teeth

Eggshell, different fizzy drinks, vinegar, bottled water, milk, screw top pots, measuring cylinders

Posters about teeth

Model teeth

Activity 2

Target group: Years 3 and 4 who are working at ARE.
Aim: To develop the skill of suggesting improvements to investigations.

What to do

Provide the children with a specific question to answer such as, 'Do fizzy drinks or non-fizzy drinks cause tooth decay?' and also the method and equipment to carry out the investigation. Model for the children what was done in the investigation. Deliberately include some mistakes that they can notice, or some vague actions. Good examples are:

- Not measuring the volumes of the liquid and using the term 'some' instead of specific measurements.
- Not measuring the mass of the eggshell and using the term 'some' instead of specific masses.
- Using different volumes of different liquids even though they are measured.
- Making vague qualitative statements as results such as 'that looks decayed'.

Discuss what the results mean and what problems there might be with the evidence, using appropriate questioning to pull out some improvements to the method. Record this on the basic evaluation mat under the sections WWW and EBI. A sample set of data can be found in the support sheet section.

Tips

- Model how we can change the question into a prediction by the sentence starter 'I think' or 'I predict' and then use the question itself.
- This can be carried out by the children, however you will need to allow time in your teaching sequence for this.

Key questions to develop the skill

- What has happened?
- Did it work?
- How difficult was it?
- What did the results mean?
- Can you answer the question?
- Would you need to do something else to answer the question?
- Was that the best way of doing that?
- Could you think of another way to answer the question?
- Which way do you think is best? Did you see any mistakes?
- Could you think of a better way of doing it?

Key vocabulary

Question stems: what, when, why, where, how

Questions, investigate, ideas, answer

Resources

A book corner filled with books on teeth

A computer open with information about teeth

Eggshell, different fizzy drinks, vinegar, bottled water, milk, screw top pots, measuring cylinders

Posters about teeth

Model teeth

Data sheet from an investigation

Activity 3

Target group: Years 3 and 4 who are working above ARE.
Aim: To develop the idea of degree of trust in data relating to the methodology and ways to improve the quality of the data.

What to do

Provide children with the method, data and conclusions from an investigation into a specific statement, such as 'Fizzy drinks cause tooth decay'. Ensure that there is a potential causal relationship within the data and that there is at least one anomalous result or outlier that doesn't fit the pattern. Ensure also that there is at least one piece of irrelevant evidence.

Discuss what the results mean and what problems there might be with the data, using appropriate questioning to pull out some improvements to the method and recording them on the basic evaluation mat. A sample set of data can be found in the support sheets section.

Now use the sequence for teaching writing; provide the children with three evaluations based upon the data (see the tooth decay evaluation sheet in the support sheets section). Ask the children to discuss the evaluations and agree on which one is the best. Now using the children's input come up with a list of rules for making a good evaluation (see Figure 5.3 above). Refer to the advanced evaluation mat to model how we make evaluative statements and the language we can use.

Formulate another question that the data could answer. Discuss it and draft it with the children, using the rules (for example: Do all fizzy drinks cause tooth decay?) Evaluation 2 is the better evaluation.

Tip

- Degrees of trust refers you to what extent the data can be used to answer the question. It deals with the accuracy and precision of results. You will notice in the method and results on the Investigating Tooth Decay Support Sheet that there are no repeats and there are some obvious errors. Do not get bogged down in terminology here, what is important is to discuss with the children why we couldn't use the results and what the issue could possibly be (for example, did the children carrying out the investigation dry the eggshell before weighing it?).

Key questions to develop the skill

- Should we agree with the statement?
- Can you spot a pattern in the results?
- Are there any results that do not fit the pattern?
- Could I trust this set of results?
- What would you suggest they do to improve their investigation?
- Why might that result not fit the pattern?
- How can you be sure that result can be used?
- Why wasn't that the best way of doing that?
- Why can I not answer the question doing it that way?
- If I were to repeat your measurements would I get the same results?
- If you were to repeat your measurements would you get the same results?
- If you were to use a different set of equipment would you get the same results?

Key vocabulary

Question stems: what, when, why, where, how

Questions, investigate, ideas, answer

Resources

Data sheet from an investigation

Sample evaluations

The final activity

Review the original launch pad activity and ask the children to amend it or add new suggestions to the sheet and any EBI. If possible, encourage them to write their own evaluation on the back of the sheet.

Give out the self-assessment sheet and ask the children to complete the second column.

Reflecting and evaluating

Years 5 and 6: Investigating insulation

Working scientifically

Working towards age-related expectations

Use results to draw simple conclusions, make predictions for new values, suggest improvements and raise further questions.

Guidance *(non-statutory)*: With support, the children should identify new questions arising from the data, making predictions for new values within or beyond the data they have collected and finding ways of improving what they have already done.

Working at age-related expectations

Report and present findings from enquiries, including conclusions, causal relationships and explanations of and **degree of trust in results, in oral and written forms such as displays and other presentations**.

Identify scientific evidence that has been used to support or refute ideas or arguments.

Use test results to make predictions to set up further comparative and fair tests.

Guidance *(non-statutory)*: They should use their results to identify when further tests and observations might be needed; recognise which secondary sources will be most useful to research their ideas and begin to separate opinion from fact.

Knowledge and understanding

Working at age-related expectations

Compare and group together everyday materials on the basis of their properties, including their hardness, solubility, transparency, conductivity (electrical and thermal), and response to magnets.

Give reasons, based on evidence from comparative and fair tests, for the particular uses of everyday materials, including metals, wood and plastic.

Mathematics

Working at age-related expectations (Year 5)

Number

Read, write, order and compare numbers to at least 1,000,000 and determine the value of each digit.

Count forwards or backwards in steps of powers of 10 for any given number up to 1,000,000.

Measurement

Convert between different units of metric measure (for example, kilometre and metre; centimetre and metre; centimetre and millimetre; gram and kilogram; litre and millilitre).

Teacher information

A property of a material is to what extent it conducts heat. If heat travels quickly it is known as a thermal conductor.

Good thermal conductors are metals. Poor thermal conductors are known as thermal insulators, for example plastic and wood. This is why they are used for saucepan handles.

Thermal conductivity or insulation is an important property to consider when using materials where energy transfer is important, such as metals. This is why metals like copper, steel and iron are used as saucepan bases.

If we wish to prevent thermal conduction we need to use insulator materials.

Launch pad

Provide the children with the method data and conclusions from an investigation sheet into insulation (not the same as below) OR use the launch pad activity with some basic data on it.

Use the questions on the sheet to guide discussion. Ask the children if they think the investigation answered the question, and if it didn't why. Then ask them to look at the method and suggest what else could be done to improve it.

Remember this is your base-line assessment so do not intervene at this point. If the children are struggling to suggest ways to find out then they can put 'I don't know' or a '?'.

Ask the children to complete the first column of the self-assessment sheet.

Activity 1

Target group: Years 5 and 6 who are working towards ARE.
Aim: To develop the skill of suggesting improvements to investigations.

What to do

Provide children with a specific question to answer such as: 'Which cup will keep a cup of hot water hot for longer?' and the method and equipment to carry out the investigation.

Model the investigation. Deliberately include some mistakes that they can notice or vague actions. Good examples are:

- Not measuring the volumes of the liquid and using the term 'some' instead of specific measurements.
- Using different volumes of different liquids even though they are measured.
- Making qualitative statements instead of measuring the temperature of the water before and after.

A set of sample data is included in the support sheets section.

Discuss what the results mean and what problems there might be with the evidence using appropriate questioning to pull out some improvements to the method. Record this on the basic evaluation mat under the sections WWW and EBI.

Tips

- Model how we can change the question into a prediction with the sentence starter 'I think' or 'I predict' and then use the question itself.
- This can be carried out by the children, however you will need to allow time in your teaching sequence for this.
- Do not place a ceiling on the comments the children make. If they come up with the idea that it is not fair then use your questioning and dialogue to explore what they mean by 'not fair'.

Key questions to develop the skill

- What has happened?
- Did it work?
- How difficult was it?
- What did the results mean?
- Can you answer the question?
- Would you need to do something else to answer the question?
- Was that the best way of doing that?
- Could you think of another way to answer the question?
- Which way do you think is best? Did you see any mistakes?
- Could you think of a better way of doing it?

Key vocabulary

Question stems: what, when, why, where, how

Questions, investigate, ideas, answer

Resources

Cups of different sizes

Cups of different materials

Source of warm water

Thermometers

Stopwatches

Sample data sheet

Activity 2

Target group: Years 5 and 6 who are working at ARE.
Aim: To develop the idea of degree of trust in data relating to the methodology and ways to improve the quality of the data.

What to do

Provide children with the method, data and conclusions from an investigation into a specific question, such as 'The diameter of the cup opening affects how long a drink stays warm'. Ensure that there is a potential causal relationship within the data and that there is at least one anomalous result or outlier that doesn't fit the pattern. Ensure also that there is at least one piece of irrelevant evidence and that there are no repeated readings. A sample data sheet is included in the support sheets section.

Discuss what the results mean and what problems there might be with the data, using appropriate questioning to pull out some of the issues. Then explore with the children possible improvements to the method.

Now use the sequence for teaching writing; provide the children with three evaluations based upon the data (see the insulation evaluation sheet in the support sheets section). Ask them to discuss the evaluations and agree on which one is the best. Now using the children's input come up with a list of rules for making a good evaluation (see Figure 5.3 above). Refer to the advanced evaluation mat to model how we make evaluative statements, explaining at each point why we use this language.

Look at your data again and formulate another question, for example, 'The more water in the cup the longer it stays hotter', and draft a conclusion with the children using the rules Evaluation 3 is the best.

Tips

- 'Degrees of trust' refers you to what extent the data can be used to answer the question. It deals with the accuracy and precision of results.
- Discuss and emphasise with the children why sometimes we cannot use results to answer a question and what the issue could possibly be with the evidence.
- Although 'diameter' is included in the Year 6 maths ARE you will need to check carefully if the children know this idea, if not you can adapt it to 'the size of the opening to the cup'.

Questions to prompt reflection and evaluation

- Should we agree with the statement?
- Can you spot a pattern in the results?
- Are there any results that do not fit the pattern?
- Could I trust this set of results?
- What would you suggest they do to improve their investigation?
- Why might that result not fit the pattern?
- How can you be sure that result can be used?
- Why wasn't that the best way of doing that?
- Why can I not answer the question doing it that way?
- If I were to repeat your measurements would I get the same results?
- If you were to repeat your measurements would you get the same?
- If you were to use a different set of equipment would you get the same results?

Key vocabulary

Question stems: what, when, why, where, how

Questions, investigate, ideas, answer

Resources

Data from an investigation

Sample evaluations

The final activity

Explore again the original launch pad task. Ask the children to annotate it based upon what they have learnt and to write their own evaluation of the investigation.

Give out the self-assessment sheet and ask the children to complete the second column.

6 Assessment

A very narrow definition of assessment is that it is judgement against a set of agreed criteria. Since the inception of the National Curriculum this has become synonymous with the term 'levels'. Levels became the benchmark to measure a child's progress and attainment and to compare schools with each other. Since the work of Black et al. at King's College in the late 1990s, the Assessment Reform Group (1999) and subsequent reforms of the National Curriculum, our knowledge and understanding of assessment, especially the value of formative assessment, has increased and this model of assessment has been called into question. The basis of the latest reforms has come from the realisation that levels came to dominate all forms of assessment and there was a deep dissatisfaction that they were not fit for purpose and were often misused. Not only were they used for both statutory National Curriculum tests and statutory reporting of teacher assessment, but they also came to be used for in-school assessment between key stages in order to monitor whether pupils were on track to achieve expected levels at the end of key stages (Commission on Assesssment Without Levels Final Report, 2015).

The latest version of the National Curriculum has addressed this by removing the requirements for levels and placing at its heart a much greater emphasis on bespoke assessment practices that contain assessment for learning and in-school assessment of learning. So what will take the place of levels? As I write this we are still in uncharted territory, but the vision of assessment for the current government is becoming clearer. The DfE has produced the following guidance for schools: 'Schools will be expected to demonstrate (with evidence) their assessment of pupils' progress, to keep parents informed, to enable governors to make judgements about the school's effectiveness, and to inform Ofsted inspections' (*Assessment Principles*, DfE 2014).

So will statutory external assessment take place for science? At this moment in time there is no plan to conduct compulsory summative assessment tests for science. However, there will be biennial sampling tests carried out at the end of KS2 to determine thresholds of 'meeting national standards'. The first new Key Stage 2 sample tests in science, based on the new National Curriculum, will be sat by pupils for the first time in the summer of 2016. They will take the format of three test papers – one each for biology, chemistry and physics contexts, ramping in difficulty as the papers progress.

The standards agency explains that the raw marks from the tests will be converted into a 'scaled score'. Next, a standard-setting exercise will be conducted on the first live test in 2016 in order to determine the scaled score needed for a pupil to be considered to have met the standard. Performance descriptors have been produced which will indicate the characteristics of the pupils who have met the national standards. Although 'Working scientifically' will be assessed in these tests, inevitably there will be areas of working scientifically that cannot be assessed via testing (see the examples in Figure 6.1). So what other assessment can take place for science in primary schools?

Years 3 and 4

Planning – asking relevant questions and using different types of scientific enquiries to answer them.

Carrying out – setting up simple practical enquiries, and comparative and fair tests.

Using test results to make predictions to set up further comparative and fair tests.

Measuring – making systematic and careful observations and, where appropriate, taking accurate measurements using standard units, using a range of equipment, including thermometers and data loggers.

Recording – gathering, recording, classifying and presenting data in a variety of ways to help in answering questions.

Reporting – reporting on findings from enquiries, including oral and written explanations, displays or presentations of results and conclusions.

Years 5 and 6

Measuring – taking measurements, using a range of scientific equipment, with increasing accuracy and precision, taking repeat readings when appropriate.

Reporting – reporting and presenting findings from enquiries, including conclusions, causal relationships and explanations of and degree of trust in results, in oral and written forms such as displays and other presentations.

Key Stage 2 Science Sampling Test Framework:
National Curriculum Tests from 2016 (DfE 2015a)

Figure 6.1 Skills that cannot easily be assessed via tests.

It is important at this stage to ensure we have a good understanding of the nature of assessment in schools as this will inform any future assessment practice in schools. Following the guidance from the DfE, the Commission on Assessment Without Levels (2015) and the NAHT, we arrive at a set of guidelines for effective assessment without levels.

Effective assessment systems:

Give reliable information to parents about how their child, and their child's school, is performing.

a Allow meaningful tracking of pupils towards end of key stage expectations in the new curriculum, including regular feedback to parents.

b Provide information which is transferable and easily understood and covers both qualitative and quantitative assessment.

c Differentiate attainment between pupils of different abilities, giving early recognition of pupils who are falling behind and those who are excelling.

d Are reliable and free from bias.

Help drive improvement for pupils and teachers.

a   Are closely linked to improving the quality of teaching.

b   Ensure feedback to pupils contributes to improved learning and is focused on specific and tangible objectives.

c   Produce recordable measures which can demonstrate comparison against expected standards and reflect progress over time.

Make sure the school is keeping up with external best practice and innovation.

a   Are created in consultation with those delivering best practice locally.

b   Are created in consideration of, and are benchmarked against, international best practice.

Assessment Principles, DfE 2014

The principles of assessment without levels

Following the recommendations of the Commission on Assessment Without Levels (2015) (an independent group of educationalists) and the work of the National Association of Head Teachers (NAHT), along with work from the TAPS project from the Primary Science Teaching Trust (2014), the situation is becoming slightly clearer and we can begin to formulate a vision for assessment without levels. Both the Commission and the NAHT have produced a set of recommendations for the establishment of assessment without the use of levels. The Commission on Assessment Without Levels (2015) recognises that assessment without levels gives schools the opportunity to develop their own innovative approaches to assessment that focus on teaching and learning and are tailored to the curriculum and followed by the school, not by a set of national standards alone. To support this, the NAHT has produced an assessment checklist which will be invaluable for anyone establishing a new assessment system. The Commission has also made the recommendation that a national bank of assessment items be developed that can be used for both formative and summative assessment.

Current models that are being used generally attempt to quantify the degree of mastery or to what extent the children have moved toward meeting ARE or national standards. As the NAHT note, schools are faced with a huge job in translating the National Curriculum ARE's descriptive statements of attainment against national standards into something workable that they can use to judge attainment. Just what evidence would be used to form these judgements is still unclear – as is the amount needed to secure the judgement. The approaches again can vary, so for some they might rely on qualitative assessment pieces that demonstrate understanding and/or skill level (my school, for example, uses 'progress books'). Some schools might choose traffic lighting against the ARE. Other schools may choose to use the sample tests or their own testing to assess achievement. Alternatively, they may choose to convert coverage of ARE into a percentage as a means to provide data for summative assessment to be used when Ofsted require evidence of progress.

Whatever system is chosen, it must follow the basic principles outlined above: it must be clear what the purpose of the assessment is, who it is for and how it will be used (being mindful of teacher workload). Only then can it be considered fit for purpose. It would, however, be a shame to waste this opportunity to create something truly innovative and bespoke for the school.

A question of evidence

In my work I have learnt the value of the range of evidence that can be used in assessment as evidence of understanding and achievement can come in many forms. I do not advocate the use of any one form of evidence and as you will see in this guide I have used the following:

Questions and answers both written and verbal.
Eavesdropping on children's discussions and taking note
Learning walls
Pre and post teaching sequence assessment
Drawings
Sorting and grouping
Self-assessment.
KWL grids

Although I haven't used them also consider the following as sources of evidence:

Observing the children and making notes
Photographing the children carrying out tasks
Photographing the outcomes of practical work
Presentations
Powerpoints

All of these can provide valuable evidence. You will of course need to find out what your setting regards as adequate evidence.

An assessment system

I believe that a system of self-assessment and a wide range of evidence of progress is at the heart of any new system for assessment. I thus provide a very simple system for you and the children to work with. Following the recommendations of the NAHT, I have chosen to work with the language of 'mastery' based on a three-step classification. First, I do not use the phrase 'working below ARE' as I feel that it is negative for the children, therefore I use the phrase 'working towards ARE' (alternative language: emerging, developing). I then use the phrase 'working at ARE' (alternative language: mastered, confident, secure, expected) and 'working above ARE'.

I will use the analogy of a rocket because after all this is science! The positive language of the rocket can be used to provide feedback for the children and provide a language of 'mastery' for teachers' records. For each skill area you will be provided with:

- **The Launch pad**. This investigation or question provides opportunities to explore the basics of the skill in a context. This will be the opportunity for the children to reflect and show what they think they know and can do. It is used as a base-line assessment and as a final comparative assessment to show progress made in the skill area.
- **Teacher assessment sheets**. I have included a set of statements based around the ARE in each skill area. These will help you break apart the ARE and give you a list of things to look for as the children work. You can then assess the Launch pad outcomes in situ by eavesdropping, by asking questions during the activity, or by assessing the written outcomes

produced by the child. This is your record of the base line and your comparison for a final assessment to show any progress. You will gain a sense of where the pupils are in relation to the ARE. There are spaces to assess progress as and when it happens and make comments, for example, in what ways the child can express their understanding. It is important at this stage to be clear for the children what evidence you will look for. I do not state how many times you can assess. This is for you to decide once you have discussed this with your school.

- **Self-assessment sheets**. These provide the children with a list of simple can do statements based on the ARE that they can check themselves against. Once the children have completed the Launch pad, they can reflect on some of the skills they have used. The self-assessment sheets are organised thus:
  - ○ *Take off* could be used with children you have assessed as below ARE.
  - ○ *Flying high* could be used with children you have assessed as working at ARE or 'mastered' the skill area.
  - ○ *Reach for the stars* could be used with children working above ARE or 'exceeding'.

The children can, with an adult or independently, work through the statements. You can either give all three stages to the children or select the one you feel is the best fit for them at that moment in time. Depending on how many of the boxes they tick (and you have witnessed) the children gain a sense of what 'stage' they are at. They can then work with you to set themselves a target, either from the existing stage or to move to the next stage.

Once you have established where the children are working in relation to the ARE you can choose your appropriate start point to develop the skill. The contextual activities I have provided allow you to either consolidate the skill or move pupils on in the skill. You teach the activities in the way that best suits your children. I deliberately do not give you a lesson plan or tell you in detail how to organise the activities, but do suggest adaptations you can make and questions that will guide dialogue with the children and challenge and develop their ideas within the skill area.

I want to emphasise that what I am suggesting is not a simple fix. The teaching of the skill should not be a one-off experience but rather a stage of a journey. Children often need multiple exposures to new skills and ways of working so this is just a starting point.

Key adaptation

If the children you are working with have special needs and it is clear that developmentally they are operating below ARE you can adapt this system. The key is to accept that some children will always be working towards their ARE and therefore we do not measure progress against 'working at' but rather to what extent they are making steps towards ARE. If this is your situation you can develop the system you choose to reflect the p levels.

Once the teaching sequence is complete you can ask the children to repeat the original Launch pad or amend or adapt their original outcomes to demonstrate what they have learnt. They will then reassess themselves using their original self-assessment sheets and set themselves further targets based on the next stage of their 'rocket journey'.

Again, I state that although I have chosen multiple statements of achievement for each strand I have not stated just how many of these statements children are to reach to demonstrate working at ARE. This is deliberate. It could be that your school will have its own threshold to quantify 'mastery' and this scheme can be adapted to that. Your school could, of course, want some form of summative assessment of progress to report to parents etc.

I would suggest that at strategic points in the year complete investigations are attempted and evaluated. These 'challenges' should be contextual and I advocate a scaffold (similar to the planning posters from the National Strategies) to prompt children to record outcomes.

I have designed the statements for self-assessment and teacher assessment to be used to give the complete picture for the teacher. You can adapt the generic self-assessment sheet for the skill to match the context example. If you were using the skill in the context of plants, for example, you could add the language of plants into the self-assessment statements as well as the generic teacher assessment sheet. You can also increase and decrease the amount of statements you wish to include.

Addendum

A recent national training event I attended made it clear to me that the existing picture of assessment is still not clear and indeed for science it is less clear than for English and maths. With no recent new directives related to science being issued from government it is still left to the individual school or collective to decide on their own assessment methods and data to collect.

Therefore to date (January 2016):

1   The principles of assessment discussed earlier still apply. It is worth emphasising again that it is up to the school what kind of assessment it carries out. It is made clear by the Commission on Assessment Without Levels Final Report (2015) that whatever form of assessment the school develops it should be meaningful and should not add to workload, especially in relation to record keeping.
2   There are still no plans for testing in science except for the sample testing the DfE will be conducting.
3   Following the *Statement on the Interim Recommendations of the Rochford Review* (2015) which makes interim recommendations of developing pre-key stage statements and the need for a review of the p levels, there is a need to think about how we assess and record progress for those pupils operating 'below national standards'.

Finally, the Association for Science Education is soon due to publish a position statement on assessment, so do check their website regularly (www.ase.org.uk).

Bibliography

Publications

ASE (1998) *Investigation for Key Stage 1 and 2: A Bank of Differentiated Investigations for Primary Schools*. Hatfield: Association for Science Education.

ASE (2010) *The Language of Measurement: Terminology Used in School Science Investigations*. Hatfield: Association for Science Education.

Commission on Assessment Without Levels Final Report (2015) www.gov.uk/government/uploads/system/uploads/attachment_data/file/461534/Commission_report_.pdf (accessed 25 February 2016).

Davies, D., Collier, C., Earle, S., Howe, A. and McMahon, K. (2014) *Approaches to Science Assessment in English Primary Schools: Interim Findings from the Teacher Assessment in Primary Science (TAPS) Project*. Bristol: Primary Science Teaching Trust.

DfE (2008) *The National Strategies (Primary): Literacy: The Teaching Sequence for Writing*. 00467-2008PDF-EN-21. London: DfE. © Crown copyright.

DfE (2013 and subsequent updates 2015) *The National Curriculum of England Framework Document.* © Crown copyright. Electronic version product code: STA/15/7344/e. London: DfE. © Crown copyright 2015. www.gov.uk/government/publications/national-curriculum-in-england-science-programmes-of-study/national-curriculum-in-england-science-programmes-of-study (accessed 25 February 2016).

DfE (April 2014) *Assessment Principles*. London: DfE. © Crown copyright.

DfE (2015a) *Key Stage 2 Science Sampling Test Framework: National Curriculum Tests from 2016.* London: DfE.

DfE (2015b) *Statement on the Interim Recommendations of the Rochford Review*. London: DfE. © Crown copyright.

DfES (2002a) *The National Strategies (Secondary Science) Literacy in Science*. 0561-2002. London: DfE. © Crown copyright.

DfES (2002b) *The National Strategies (Secondary Science) Scientific Enquiry Posters*. 0495/2002. London: DfE. © Crown copyright.

Driver, R., Leach, J., Millar, R. and Scott, P. (1996) *Young People's Images of Science*. Maidenhead: Oxford University Press.

Goldsworthy, A. and Feasey, R. (1997) *Making Sense of Primary Science Investigations*. Hatfield: Association for Science Education.

Goldsworthy, A. and Ponchaud, B. (2007) *Science Enquiry Games*. Sandbach, Cheshire: Millgate House Publishers.

Goldsworthy, A., Watson, J.R. and Wood-Robinson, V. (2000) *Getting to Grips with Graphs*. Hatfield: Science Teacher Education.

Gott, R., Duggan, S., Roberts, R. and Hussain, A. (2015) *Research into Understanding Scientific Evidence*. University of Durham. http://community.dur.ac.uk/rosalyn.roberts/Evidence/cofev.htm. (accessed 25 February 2016).

Harlen, W. (ed.) (2005) *ASE Guide To Primary Science Education*. Hatfield: Association for Science Education.

Harlen, W. and Qualter, A. (2015) *The Teaching of Science in Primary Schools*. Abingdon: Routledge.

Johnston, J. (2009) Observation as an important enquiry skill. *ASE Primary Science,* 106, pp. 15–17.

NAHT Assessment Design Checklist, www.naht.org.uk/ (accessed 25 February 2016).

NAHT Assessment Framework, www.naht.org.uk/ (accessed 25 February 2016).

NAHT Commission on Assessment Without Levels, www.naht.org.uk/welcome/news-and-media/ key-topics/assessment/profession-takes-lead-on-assessment-after-the-end-of-levels/ (accessed 25 February 2016).

Ofsted (January 2011) *Successful Science*. London: Ofsted. © Crown copyright.

Ofsted (November 2013) *Maintaining Curiosity: A Survey in Science Education in Schools*. 130135. London: Ofsted. © Crown copyright.

QCDA (2009) *Assessing Pupil Progress in Primary Science* (2009). 01063-2009PDF-EN-05. London: QCDA. © Crown copyright.

Online resources

Cambridge Assessment, Tim Oates, 'Life Without Levels in Depth' podcast, www. cambridgeassessment.org.uk/insights/assessment-without-levels-extended-version-tim-oates-insights/

Science & Plants for Schools (2007a) 'Growing plants in a classroom' guide, www.saps.org.uk/ attachments/article/236/Living_Processes_PartC.pdf

Science & Plants for Schools (2007b) 'How fast does a root grow?' teacher's resource, www. saps.org.uk/primary/teaching-resources/217-how-fast-does-a-root-grow

STEM Learning, Scientific Enquiry posters, www.nationalstemcentre.org.uk/elibrary/ resource/5327/scientific-enquiry-training-materials

Further reading

Assessment Reform Group (1999) *Assessment for Learning: Beyond the Black Box.* Cambridge: University of Cambridge.

Black, P. and Wiliam, D. (1998) *Inside the Black Box: Raising Standards through Classroom Assessment*. London: King's College London.

Black, P., Harrison, C., Lee, C., Marshall, B. and Wiliam, D. (2002) *Working Inside the Black Box: Assessment for Learning in the Classroom*. London: King's College London.

Howe, A. and McMahon, K. (2014) *Approaches to Science Assessment in English Primary Schools*. Bath: Centre for Research in Early Scientific Learning (CRESL), Bath Spa University. www.bathspa.ac.uk/schools/education/research-in-education/research-projects/cresl-teacher-assessment-in-primary-years (accessed 25 February 2016).

King's College London, CASE project, www.kcl.ac.uk/sspp/departments/education/research/ crestem/Research/Past-Projects/Cognaccel.aspx (accessed 25 February 2016).

Primary Science Teaching Trust (formerly Astrazenica Teaching Trust), *Outcomes from Research.* www.pstt.org.uk/resources/curriculum-materials.aspx (accessed 25 February 2016).

SCORE – Science Community Representing Education. *Practical Work in Primary Science.* www.score-education.org

Toplis, R. (ed.) (2010) *How Science Works: Exploring Effective Pedagogy and Practice*. Abingdon: Routledge.

Turner, J. (2012) 'It's not fair', *ASE Primary Science*, 121, 30–33.

Welsh Assembly Government (2010) *Developing Higher-Order Scientific Enquiry Skills*. http:// oer.educ.cam.ac.uk/wiki/Developing_Higher_Order_Scientific_Enquiry_Skills (accessed 25 February 2016).

Appendices

Appendix 1 Self-assessment sheets

Planning self-assessment
Years 1 and 2

How successful have you been at planning? How could you be even better at it?

I am flying high

What I can do	1st	2nd	What I can do	1st	2nd
I can ask a question about something I have seen			I can try a different way to answer my question		
I can ask more than one question about something I have seen			I can do what my teacher suggested to find the answer to my question		
I can think of something I can do to help me answer my question			With a bit of help from my teacher, I can choose a way to answer my question		

To be even better at planning I need to …

Planning self-assessment
Years 1 and 2

How successful have you been at planning? How could you be even better at it?

I am reaching for the stars

What I can do	1st	2nd	What I can do	1st	2nd
I can ask a question that can be answered by an investigation			I can suggest my own way of answering a question		
I can ask a question beginning with the word 'what?' that I can investigate			I can decide what is the best way to answer the question		
I can ask a question beginning with the word 'why?' that I can investigate			I can show or tell my teacher what is the best equipment to use to answer my question		
I can ask a question beginning with the word 'when?' that I can investigate			I can tell my teacher if I think the way to answer the question will work or not		
I can ask a question beginning with the word 'where?' that I can investigate			I can use an observation investigation to help me answer a question		
I can tell if my question is a good one to ask			I can use a research investigation to help me answer a question		
I can try one way to answer my question			I can use a fair test investigation to answer a question		
I can suggest a different way to answer my question			I can think of some more questions to ask once I have finished my investigation		
I can try a different way to answer my question			I can make a new prediction based on what I have found out		

To be even better at planning I need to …

Planning self-assessment
Years 3 and 4

How successful have you been at planning? How could you be even better at it?

I am taking off

What I can do	1st	2nd	What I can do	1st	2nd
I can ask a question about something I have seen			I can try a different way to answer my question		
I can ask more than one question about something I have seen			I can do what my teacher suggested to find the answer to my question		
I can think of something to do to answer my question			With a bit of help from my teacher, I can choose a way to answer my question		

To be even better at planning I need to …

Planning self-assessment
Years 3 and 4

How successful have you been at planning? How could you be even better at it?

I am flying high

What I can do	1st	2nd	What I can do	1st	2nd
I can ask a question that can be answered by an investigation			I can suggest my own way of answering a question		
I can ask a question beginning with the word 'what?' that I can investigate			I can decide what is the best way to answer the question		
I can ask a question beginning with the word 'why?' that I can investigate			I can show or tell my teacher what is the best equipment to use to answer my question		
I can ask a question beginning with the word 'when?' that I can investigate			I can tell my teacher if I think the way to answer the question will work or not		
I can ask a question beginning with the word 'where?' that I can investigate			I can use an observation investigation to help me answer a question		
I can tell if my question is a good one to ask			I can use a research investigation to help me answer a question		
I can try one way to answer my question			I can use a fair test investigation to answer a question		
I can suggest a different way to answer my question			I can think of some more questions to ask once I have finished my investigation		
I can try a different way to answer my question			I can make a new prediction based on what I have found out		

To be even better at planning I need to …

Planning self-assessment
Years 3 and 4

How successful have you been at planning? How could you be even better at it?

I am reaching for the stars

What I can do	1st	2nd	What I can do	1st	2nd
I can suggest a way to answer a question			I can reject ways to answer a question that will not work		
I can plan a way to answer a question			I can say why I think something will not give me an answer		
I can choose the best way to answer my question			I can identify questions that need a fair test enquiry		
I can plan an observation enquiry			I can phrase my question in a way that helps me know how to answer it		
I can plan a research investigation			Without help I can select the equipment I need to use		
I can plan a fair test investigation			Without help I can say what I need to measure and how many times		
I can plan a pattern-seeking investigation			I can say why my observations will be accurate		
I can identify the variable I need to change			I can say why my observations will be precise		
I can identify the variables I need to keep the same			I can think of a new fair test investigation to carry out based on what I have found out in my first investigation		
I can identify the variable that I will measure or observe			I can use my test results to predict what will happen in a new investigation		

Planning self-assessment
Years 5 and 6

How successful have you been at planning? How could you be even better at it?

I am taking off

What I can do	1st	2nd	What I can do	1st	2nd
I can ask a question that can be answered by an investigation			I can suggest my own way of answering a question		
I can ask a question beginning with the word 'what?' that I can investigate			I can decide what was the best way to answer the question		
I can ask a question beginning with the word 'why?' that I can investigate			I can show or tell my teacher what is the best equipment to use to answer my question		
I can ask a question beginning with the word 'when?' that I can investigate			I can tell my teacher if I think the way to answer the question will work or not		
I can ask a question beginning with the word 'where?' that I can investigate			I can use an observation investigation to help me answer a question		
I can tell if my question is a good one to ask			I can use a research investigation to help me answer a question		
I can try one way to answer my question			I can use a fair test investigation to answer a question		
I can suggest a different way to answer my question			I can think of some more questions to ask once I have finished my investigation		
I can try a different way to answer my question			I can make a new prediction based on what I have found out		

To be even better at planning I need to …

Planning self-assessment
Years 5 and 6

How successful have you been at planning? How could you be even better at it?

I am flying high

What I can do	1st	2nd	What I can do	1st	2nd
I can suggest a way to answer a question			I can reject ways to answer a question that will not work		
I can plan a way to answer a question			I can say why I think something will not give me an answer		
I can choose the best way to answer my question			I can identify questions that need a fair test enquiry		
I can plan an observation enquiry			I can phrase my question in a way that helps me know how to answer it		
I can plan a research investigation			Without help I can select the equipment I need to use		
I can plan a fair test investigation			Without help I can say what I need to measure and how many times		
I can plan a pattern-seeking investigation			I can say why my observations will be accurate		
I can identify the variable I need to change			I can say why my observations will be precise		
I can identify the variables I need to keep the same			I can think of a new fair test investigation to carry out based on what I have found out in my first investigation		
I can identify the variable that I will measure or observe			I can use my test results to predict what will happen in a new investigation		

To be even better at planning I need to …

Observation self-assessment
Years 1 and 2

How successful have you been at observing? How could you be even better at it?

I am flying high

What I can do	1st	2nd	What I can do	1st	2nd
I can choose what I want to observe			I can draw what I see		
I can describe how big or small something is			I can use rulers to measure something		
I can describe shapes			I can use egg timers to measure time		
I can describe sizes			I can use magnifying glasses/ hand lenses to look at something		
I can describe colours			I can say how something has changed over time		
I can describe textures			I can take photographs of things I notice		
I can describe smells			I can collect something I notice		

To be even better at observing I need to …

Observation self-assessment
Years 1 and 2

How successful have you been at observing? How could you be even better at it?

I am reaching for the stars

What I can do	1st	2nd	What I can do	1st	2nd
I can measure length in cm with a ruler			With a bit of help I can decide what I want to observe to answer my question		
I can measure length in mm with a ruler			With a bit of help I can decide what equipment I need to make my observation		
I can measure mass using a spring balance			With a bit of help I can make accurate measurements		
I can measure mass in g using a digital balance			With a bit of help I can decide how long I want to observe something for		
I decide to use a mm ruler to make a very small measurement			With a bit of help I can present my observations in the best way to answer my question		
I decide to use a metre ruler to make a very big measurement			I can draw a simple table or tally chart to record what I find out		
I can use a stopwatch to measure time in s			I can use a simple graph or chart to show my results		
I can use a data logger with a probe to measure something			I use the correct units when I record a measurement		
I can measure temperature using a thermometer			My measurements match everyone else's in the class		

To be even better at observing I need to …

Observation self-assessment
Years 3 and 4

How successful have you been at observing? How could you be even better at it?

I am taking off

What I can do	1st	2nd	What I can do	1st	2nd
I can choose what I want to observe			I can draw what I see		
I can say how big or small something is			I can use rulers to measure something		
I can describe shapes			I can use egg timers to measure time		
I can describe sizes			I can use magnifying glasses/ hand lenses to look at something		
I can describe colours			I can say how something has changed over time		
I can describe textures			I can take photographs of things I notice		
I can describe smells			I can collect something I notice		

To be even better at observing I need to …

Observation self-assessment
Years 3 and 4

How successful have you been at observing? How could you be even better at it?

I am flying high

What I can do	1st	2nd	What I can do	1st	2nd
I can measure length in cm with a ruler			With a bit of help I can decide what I want to observe to answer my question		
I can measure length in mm with a ruler			With a bit of help I can decide what equipment I need to make my observation		
I can measure mass using a spring balance			With a bit of help I can make accurate measurements		
I can measure mass in g using a digital balance			With a bit of help I can decide how long I want to observe something for		
I decide to use a mm ruler to make a very small measurement			With a bit of help I can present my observations in the best way to answer my question		
I decide to use a metre ruler to make a very big measurement			I can draw a simple table or tally chart to record what I find out		
I can use a stopwatch to measure time in s			I can use a simple graph or chart to show my results		
I can use a data logger with a probe to measure something			I use the correct units when I record a measurement		
I can measure temperature using a thermometer			My measurements match everyone else's in the class		

To be even better at observing I need to …

Observation self-assessment
Years 3 and 4

How successful have you been at observing? How could you be even better at it?

I am reaching for the stars

What I can do	1st	2nd	What I can do	1st	2nd
I can decide what observations I want to make			I can decide the best way to present my observations to someone		
I can decide what equipment I want to use to measure			I can record my observations in a table		
I can decide what units I want to measure in			I can record my observations in a bar chart		
I can decide how many times to measure something			I can record my observations in a line graph		
I can decide how long to observe something for			I can record my observations in a diagram		
I don't make many mistakes when I am using equipment to measure			I can tell or show someone else how to be precise		
I can show someone else how to use a piece of equipment to measure something accurately			I can use the correct scientific words to describe my observations		
I can use a range of equipment to measure things			I can record my observations using the correct units		

Observation self-assessment
Years 5 and 6

How successful have you been at observing? How could you be even better at it?

I am taking off

What I can do	1st	2nd	What I can do	1st	2nd
I can measure length in cm with a ruler			With a bit of help I can decide what I want to observe to answer my question		
I can measure length in mm with a ruler			With a bit of help I can decide what equipment I need to make my observation		
I can measure mass using a spring balance			With a bit of help I can make accurate measurements		
I can measure mass in g using a digital balance			With a bit of help I can decide how long I want to observe something for		
I decide to use a mm ruler to make a very small measurement			With a bit of help I can present my observations in the best way to answer my question		
I decide to use a metre ruler to make a very big measurement			I can draw a simple table or tally chart to record what I find out		
I can use a stopwatch to measure time in s			I can use a simple graph or chart to show my results		
I can use a data logger with a probe to measure something			I use the correct units when I record a measurement		
I can measure temperature using a thermometer			My measurements match everyone else's in the class		

To be even better at observing I need to …

Observation self-assessment
Years 5 and 6

How successful have you been at observing? How could you be even better at it?

I am flying high

What I can do	1st	2nd	What I can do	1st	2nd
I can decide what observations I want to make			I can decide the best way to present my observations to someone		
I can decide what equipment I want to use to measure			I can record my observations in a table		
I can decide what units I want to measure in			I can record my observations in a bar chart		
I can decide how many times to measure something			I can record my observations in a line graph		
I can decide how long to observe something for			I can record my observations in a diagram		
I don't make many mistakes when I am using equipment to measure			I can tell or show someone else how to be precise		
I can show someone else how to use a piece of equipment to measure something accurately			I can use the correct scientific words to describe my observations		
I can use a range of equipment to measure things			I can record my observations using the correct units		

To be even better at observing I need to …

Concluding self-assessment
Years 1 and 2

How successful have you been at concluding? How could you be even better at it?

I am flying high

What I can do	1st	2nd	What I can do	1st	2nd
I give an answer to my question			I can use something I measured to help me answer my question		
I can use something I have observed to help me answer my question			I can talk about what I have found out		
I can use something I have found out to help me answer my question			I can talk about how I found an answer to my question		

To be even better at concluding I need to …

Concluding self-assessment
Years 1 and 2

How successful have you been at concluding? How could you be even better at it?

I am reaching for the stars

What I can do	1st	2nd	What I can do	1st	2nd
I can write down what I have found out			I can identify a simple pattern from the similarities in the results		
I can draw what I have found out			I can identify the differences between results		
I can tell my teacher what I have found out			I can say if there isn't a pattern in the results		
I can use one of my observations to help me make a conclusion			I can use the pattern in my results to help me answer the question		
I can use some of the correct scientific words to explain what my evidence means			I can say if my results can't be used to answer the question I am investigating		
I can use some correct scientific words to answer my question			I can use what I have found out to ask a different question		
I can use some scientific ideas to explain what I have found out			I can use what I have found out to make a new prediction		

To be even better at concluding I need to …

Concluding self-assessment
Years 3 and 4

How successful have you been at concluding? How could you be even better at it?

I am taking off

What I can do	1st	2nd	What I can do	1st	2nd
I give an answer to my question			I can use something I measured to help me answer my question		
I can use something I have observed to help me answer my question			I can talk about what I have found out		
I can use something I have found out to help me answer my question			I can talk about how I found an answer to my question		

To be even better at concluding I need to …

Concluding self-assessment
Years 3 and 4

How successful have you been at concluding? How could you be even better at it?

I am flying high

What I can do	1st	2nd	What I can do	1st	2nd
I can write down what I have found out			I can identify a simple pattern from the similarities in the results		
I can draw what I have found out			I can identify the differences between results		
I can tell my teacher what I have found out			I can say if there isn't a pattern in the results		
I can use one of my observations to help me make a conclusion			I can use the pattern in my results to help me answer the question		
I can use some of the correct scientific words to explain what my evidence means			I can say if my results can't be used to answer the question I am investigating		
I can use some correct scientific words to answer my question			I can use what I have found out to ask a different question		
I can use some scientific ideas to explain what I have found out			I can use what I have found out to make a new prediction		

To be even better at concluding I need to …

Concluding self-assessment
Years 3 and 4

How successful have you been at concluding? How could you be even better at it?

I am reaching for the stars

What I can do	1st	2nd	What I can do	1st	2nd
I can make a conclusion using all my evidence that is relevant to the question asked			I can identify a piece of evidence I can use to say why my original idea was wrong		
I can use a range of my evidence to say why something happened			I can identify the evidence I can use to say why my question cannot be answered this way		
I can use a relevant scientific idea to explain why something should happen			I can say how much I trust what I have found out		
I can use both a relevant scientific idea and my evidence to answer my question			I can use the term 'fair' when thinking about my evidence		
I can say if my evidence is good enough to be used in my answer			I can use the term 'accurate' when discussing my evidence		
I can identify what evidence I have that supports my conclusion			I can use the term 'precise' when discussing my evidence		
I can identify what evidence I have that does not support the conclusion			I can use my evidence to make a new prediction and say why my original prediction had to change		

Concluding self-assessment
Years 5 and 6

How successful have you been at concluding? How could you be even better at it?

I am taking off

What I can do	1st	2nd	What I can do	1st	2nd
I can write down what I have found out			I can identify a simple pattern from the similarities in the results		
I can draw what I have found out			I can identify the differences between results		
I can tell my teacher what I have found out			I can say if there isn't a pattern in the results		
I can use one of my observations to help me make a conclusion			I can use the pattern in my results to help me answer the question		
I can use some of the correct scientific words to explain what my evidence means			I can say if my results can't be used to answer the question I am investigating		
I can use some correct scientific words to answer my question			I can use what I have found out to ask a different question		
I can use some scientific ideas to explain what I have found out			I can use what I have found out to make a new prediction		

To be even better at concluding I need to ...

Concluding self-assessment
Years 5 and 6

How successful have you been at concluding? How could you be even better at it?

I am flying high

What I can do	1st	2nd	What I can do	1st	2nd
I can make a conclusion using all my evidence that is relevant to the question asked			I can identify a piece of evidence I can use to say why my original idea was wrong		
I can use a range of my evidence to say why something happened			I can identify the evidence I can use to say why my question cannot be answered this way		
I can use a relevant scientific idea to explain why something should happen			I can say how much I trust what I have found out		
I can use both a relevant scientific idea and my evidence to answer my question			I can use the term 'fair' when thinking about my evidence		
I can say if my evidence is good enough to be used in my answer			I can use the term 'accurate' when discussing my evidence		
I can identify what evidence I have that supports my conclusion			I can use the term 'precise' when discussing my evidence		
I can identify what evidence I have that does not support the conclusion			I can use my evidence to make a new prediction and say why my original prediction had to change		

To be even better at concluding I need to …

Evaluating self-assessment
Years 1 and 2

How successful have you been at evaluating? How could you be even better at it?

I am flying high

What I can do	1st	2nd	What I can do	1st	2nd
I can say if I answered my question			I can say if I could have used anything else to answer my question		
I can say if anything unexpected happened			I can say if I made any mistakes in my work		
I can describe anything unexpected that happened			I can say if I worked well in a team		
I can say what I used to answer my question					

To be even better at evaluating I need to …

Evaluating self-assessment
Years 1 and 2

How successful have you been at evaluating? How could you be even better at it?

I am reaching for the stars

What I can do	1st	2nd	What I can do	1st	2nd
I can say if I answered my question			I can suggest a way to improve my working		
I can identify and describe any unexpected results			I can describe something to do to improve my results		
I can identify any patterns I used to answer my question			I can say if I could have used any other evidence to answer my question		
I can identify any results that don't fit my pattern			I can suggest another question I could answer using my results		
I can say if my results are good enough to answer my question					

To be even better at evaluating I need to …

Evaluating self-assessment
Years 3 and 4

How successful have you been at evaluating? How could you be even better at it?

I am taking off

What I can do	1st	2nd	What I can do	1st	2nd
I can say if I answered my question			I can say if I could have used anything else to answer my question		
I can say if anything unexpected happened			I can say if I made any mistakes in my work		
I can describe anything unexpected that happened			I can say if I worked well in a team		
I can say what I used to answer my question					

To be even better at evaluating I need to …

Evaluating self-assessment
Years 3 and 4

How successful have you been at evaluating? How could you be even better at it?

I am flying high

What I can do	1st	2nd	What I can do	1st	2nd
I can say if I answered my question			I can suggest a way to improve my working		
I can identify and describe any unexpected results			I can describe something to do to improve my results		
I can identify any patterns I used to answer my question			I can say if I could have used any other evidence to answer my question		
I can identify any results that don't fit my pattern			I can suggest another question I could answer using my results		
I can say if my results are good enough to answer my question					

To be even better at evaluating I need to ...

Evaluating self-assessment
Years 3 and 4

How successful have you been at evaluating? How could you be even better at it?

I am reaching for the stars

What I can do	1st	2nd	What I can do	1st	2nd
I can say if my investigation was fair			I can suggest a way to make my results more accurate		
I can say if my results were accurate			I can suggest a way to check if my results are precise		
I can describe the ways my results are similar or different to those obtained by someone else			I can suggest a new way of carrying out the investigation that can give more trustworthy results		
I can identify any results that do not fit the pattern I have identified			I can suggest a new question to be investigated based on my results		
I can say if I can trust my results or not			I can suggest a new prediction based on my results		
I can explain why I do or do not trust my results					
I can suggest a way to make my investigation fairer					

To be even better at evaluating I need to …

Evaluating self-assessment
Years 5 and 6

How successful have you been at evaluating? How could you be even better at it?

I am taking off

What I can do	1st	2nd	What I can do	1st	2nd
I can say if I answered my question			I can suggest a way to improve my working		
I can identify and describe any unexpected results			I can describe something to do to improve my results		
I can identify any patterns I used to answer my question			I can say if I could have used any other evidence to answer my question		
I can identify any results that don't fit my pattern			I can suggest another question I could answer using my results		
I can say if my results are good enough to answer my question					

To be even better at evaluating I need to …

Evaluating self-assessment
Years 5 and 6

How successful have you been at evaluating? How could you be even better at it?

I am flying high

What I can do	1st	2nd	What I can do	1st	2nd
I can say if my investigation was fair			I can suggest a way to make my results more accurate		
I can say if my results were accurate			I can suggest a way to check if my results are precise		
I can describe the ways my results are similar or different to those obtained by someone else			I can suggest a new way of carrying out the investigation that can give more trustworthy results		
I can identify any results that do not fit the pattern I have identified			I can suggest a new question to be investigated based on my results		
I can say if I can trust my results or not			I can suggest a new prediction based on my results		
I can explain why I do or do not trust my results					
I can suggest a way to make my investigation fairer					

Appendix 2 Teacher assessment sheets

Teacher assessment: Questioning, predicting and planning

ARE	Skill	Attempt 1	Attempt 2	Attempt 3	Comments
1+2	Asks a question about something they have seen, experienced, read or heard				
1+2	Asks more than one question about something they have seen, experienced, read or heard				
1+2	Attempts to answer the question based on their own experience				
1+2	Suggests/demonstrates a way to find out an answer to a question				
1+2	Follows a suggestion to find an answer to a question				
1+2	Chooses a way of answering a question from a range of options				
3+4	Asks a suitable question that can be answered				
3+4	Asks a range of questions that require different investigative methods				
3+4	Demonstrates awareness of the suitability of questions and how easy they are to investigate				
3+4	Suggests an answer to their question before they attempt their investigation				
3+4	Attempts more than one method to answer a question (can be provided by the teacher)				
3+4	Can identify/choose the best way to answer the question				
3+4	Can carry out an 'observation over time' investigation to answer a question				
3+4	Can carry out a research investigation to answer a question				

© 2016, *Working Scientifically*, Kevin Smith, Routledge

ARE	Skill	Attempt 1	Attempt 2	Attempt 3	Comments
3+4	Can carry out a simple fair test investigation to answer a question				
3+4	Can suggest what was changed and what has changed in the investigation				
3+4	Can recognise when a fair test is needed to answer the question				
3+4	Can carry out an identification and classification investigation to answer a question				
3+4	Can carry out a pattern-seeking investigation to answer a question				
3+4	Makes suggestions on how to set up an investigation				
5+6	Based on prior science experience independently suggests a suitable question that can be investigated				
5+6	Based on prior science experience independently can change a question into an investigable form				
5+6	Based on prior science experience suggests a suitable answer to their question				
5+6	Based on prior science experience attempts to give a reason why they have made a prediction				
5+6	Based on prior science experience independently suggests a suitable approach to answer the question				
5+6	Correctly identifies when a fair or comparative test is necessary to answer the question				
5+6	Can recognise and identify variables				
5+6	Can suggest what variables need to be controlled				
5+6	Can suggest the independent variable and how it should be changed				
5+6	Can suggest the dependent variable and how it should be measured				
5+6	Can explain why it is necessary to control the variables in a fair test investigation				
5+6	Uses the language of variables confidently				

Teacher assessment : Observing and recording evidence

ARE	Skill	Attempt 1	Attempt 2	Attempt 3	Comments
1+2	Chooses what they want to observe (may or may not be relevant)				
1+2	Describes how big/small something is				
1+2	Describes shapes				
1+2	Describes sizes				
1+2	Describes colours				
1+2	Describes textures				
1+2	Describes smells				
1+2	Draws what they see				
1+2	Uses rulers to measure something				
1+2	Uses egg timers to measure time				
1+2	Uses magnifying glasses/hand lenses to look at something and describe it				
1+2	Describes/says/shows how something has changed over time				
1+2	Records results in prepared table/format				
1+2	Takes photographs of things noticed				
1+2	Collects something they notice				
3+4	Can measure length in cm with a ruler				
3+4	Can measure length in mm with a ruler				

ARE	Skill	Attempt 1	Attempt 2	Attempt 3	Comments
3+4	Their measurements of length of the same object match another				
3+4	Can measure mass using a spring balance				
3+4	Can measure mass using a digital balance				
3+4	Can use a mm ruler to make a relevant measurement				
3+4	Can use a metre ruler to make a relevant measurement				
3+4	Can use a stopwatch to measure time				
3+4	Can use a data logger with a probe to measure something				
3+4	Can measure temperature using a thermometer				
3+4	With help makes accurate measurements				
3+4	With help decides what they want to observe to answer my question				
3+4	With help decides what equipment they need to make their observation				
3+4	With help decides how long they want to observe something for				
3+4	With help they can present their observations in the best way to answer their question				
3+4	Draws a simple table or tally chart to record what they find out				
3+4	Uses the correct units when they record a measurement				
3+4	Follows instructions to use a less familiar piece of equipment to measure				
5+6	Decides what observations they want to make				
5+6	Decides what equipment they want to use to measure				
5+6	Decides what units they want to measure in				
5+6	Decides how to check the precision of their measurements (by repeating)				
5+6	Decides how long to observe something for				

ARE	Skill	Attempt 1	Attempt 2	Attempt 3	Comments
5+6	Readings are made with a suitable degree of accuracy for the task				
5+6	Demonstrates how to measure something accurately				
5+6	Decides the best way to present observations to someone				
5+6	Records observations in a table that they've drawn themselves				
5+6	Records observations in a bar chart				
5+6	Records observations in a line graph				
5+6	Records observations in a diagram				
5+6	Explains or shows someone else how to be accurate				
5+6	Uses the correct scientific words to describe the observations				
5+6	Uses the correct units to record an observation				

Teacher assessment: Interpreting, analysing and concluding

ARE	Skill	Attempt 1	Attempt 2	Attempt 3	Comments
1+2	Tries to use a piece of evidence to answer the question that may or may not be relevant				
1+2	Tries to answer their question				
1+2	Tries to use an idea that may or may not be relevant to answer the question				
1+2	Answers the original question in a simple yes/no format				
1+2	Suggests an answer which may or may not be relevant				
3+4	Can present (in a suitable format) what they have found out				
3+4	Writes down what they have found out				
3+4	Draws what they have found out				
3+4	Can tell you what they have found out				
3+4	Uses one thing they have found out to make a simple conclusion about what they were investigating				
3+4	Uses what they have found out to make a different and new prediction				
3+4	Uses what they have found out to say what they can do to improve the investigation				
3+4	Uses what they have found out to ask a new question to be investigated				
3+4	Uses some scientific words related to the evidence to describe what they have found out and what it means				

ARE	Skill	Attempt 1	Attempt 2	Attempt 3	Comments
3+4	Uses some scientific words related to the evidence to answer the question they were investigating				
3+4	Can identify a simple pattern from the similarities in the results				
3+4	Can identify the differences between results				
3+4	Can say if there isn't a pattern in the results				
3+4	Can relate the pattern to the original question and say if it can be used to answer it				
3+4	Attempts to use the scientific idea to answer the question				
5+6	Makes a suitable conclusion based on their evidence				
5+6	Where there is evidence of causality can express this in a suitable format				
5+6	Can use the appropriate scientific idea and evidence to answer their original question				
5+6	Says if the evidence is good enough to answer the question				
5+6	Identifies what evidence they have that supports the conclusion				
5+6	Identifies what evidence they have that does not support the conclusion				
5+6	Can identify a piece of evidence they can use to refute a claim				
5+6	Says to what extent they trust the results				
5+6	May be able to use the term 'fair' in the correct way to discuss their evidence				
5+6	May be able to use the term 'reliable' to discuss their evidence				

Teacher assessment: Reflecting and evaluating

ARE	Skill	Attempt 1	Attempt 2	Attempt 3	Comments
1+2	Says if their findings answer my question or not				
1+2	Says if what happened was what they expected to happen				
1+2	Describes any unexpected events or outcomes				
1+2	Says if the way they chose to investigate answered the question				
3+4	Describes a way to improve the way they worked				
3+4	Uses what they have found out to say what they can do to improve their investigation				
3+4	Uses what they have found out to ask a new question to be investigated				
3+4	Identifies any evidence that doesn't fit a pattern				
3+4	Says if the evidence is good enough to answer their question				
3+4	Identifies what evidence they have that supports their conclusion				
3+4	Identifies what evidence they have that does not support their conclusion				
5+6	Identifies any issues with fairness (if a fair test investigation)				
5+6	Identifies any issues with accuracy/precision				
5+6	Says to what extent they trust the evidence				
5+6	Says why the evidence cannot be trusted/used (uses terminology of accuracy and precision)				

ARE	Skill	Attempt 1	Attempt 2	Attempt 3	Comments
5+6	Identifies any inconsistencies in the data that means they cannot trust their data				
5+6	Makes suggestions on how to improve accuracy				
5+6	Makes suggestions on how to check precision (repeating tests)				
5+6	Uses their findings to suggest a new way of answering the question				
5+6	Uses the findings to suggest a new prediction that they can investigate				
5+6	Uses the findings to formulate a new question that can be investigated				

Appendix 3 Planning mats

My basic planning mat

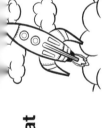

Words I can use to start a question

What?
When?
How?
Who?
Why?
Where?

Words I can use to connect

Does
Did
Is
Are
Was
Will
Would
Could

What is it I am looking at? What is it I am doing?

These are my questions:

My final question is …

What I need to find out …

What could I do to answer my question?

What can I do to answer my question?
Observe over time

See if there is a pattern

See if I can group things

Do a fair test

Do some research?

My advanced planning mat

My question is:

Words to start my question
What? When? How?
Why? Where? Does?

Things I can change (independent variables)

What I will change
How I will change it

Prediction phrases
I think
When I
When the
Will
Will not
Increase
Decrease
Go up
Go down

Things I can keep the same (control variables)

What I will keep the same to make it fair

Things I can measure/observe (dependent variables)

I will measure …
How I will measure it

Measurements
Length in cm or m
Mass in g or kg
Volume in ml or l
Time in s or mins

What I think will happen …

My basic observation mat

My observation words

Size words
long, short, narrow, wide, big, small, medium, large

Colour words
brown, grey, green, orange, red,
blue, black, white, yellow, purple

Shape words
box, round, cone, triangle, square, rectangle

Texture words
rough, smooth, spikey

Properties words
hard, soft, transparent,
translucent, opaque, bendy, brittle, flexible, stretchy,
waterproof, shiny, dull, reflective

Smell words
sweet, woody, sour, smelly

Taste words
sweet, bitter, sour, salty, acid

The question I am trying to answer is …

What I have observed is …

My observation equipment

my eyes, my ears, my nose, my fingers, my tongue,
hand lens, magnifying glass, ruler, stopwatch,
scales, data logger, sound meter, light meter

My observations numbers/units

mm = millimetres
cm = centimetres
m = metres
g = grams
kg = kilograms
s = seconds
min = minutes
h = hours

My advanced observation mat

These are my observations:

My observation equipment

My measurements

My tips for accuracy and precision
To make my observations more accurate I will …

To make my observations more precise I will …

My basic concluding mat

My pattern

My question I want to answer is …

The answer to my question is …

My piece of evidence I want to use is …

Because …

My evidence

My advanced concluding mat

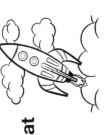

Evidence words and phrases

measurements
evidence
data
results
increase
decrease
stays the same
accurate
precise
trust
repeat

My question I want to answer is …

My conclusion is …

Concluding and analysing words

pattern
conclusion
bigger/smaller
faster/slower
increased/decreased
stayed the same

Concluding phrases

I can conclude
My conclusion is
As I increased
As I decreased
The more I
The less I
This is because

My basic evaluation mat

Reflection and evaluation words and phrases

yes/no
right/wrong
good/bad
It worked/didn't work
I can make it better
I could do …
I needed to ….
Another way to do it …
A different way …
The best way…
The worse way …
observations
evidence
questions
predictions
safer
quicker
slower
accurate
precise
fair

The question is:

Could I answer the question?

How did I answer the question?

What went well in the investigation?

The way I worked

Even better if …

My method

Even better if …

My results

Even better if …

My advanced evaluation mat

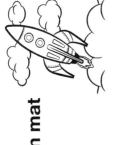

My conclusion is …

My evaluation is …

My suggestions for improvement are …

Reflection and evaluation words and phrases

questions, predictions, assess, choose, conclude, criticise, decide, determine, disagree, estimate, evidence, evaluate, judge, justify, measure, compare, recommend, select, agree, interpret, explain, opinion, support, prove, disprove, accurate, precise, fair, safer
It worked/didn't work
I can make it better
I could do …
I needed to …
Another way to do it …
A different way …
The best way …
The worse way …

Connectives

therefore, however, but, so, as a consequence, because

Appendix 4 Launch pad activities

Planning, Years 1 and 2: Launch pad

What is the weather like today?

What would you like to know about the weather?
Let's think of some questions.

How could you find that out?

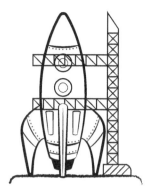

Planning, Years 3 and 4: Launch pad

Let's make some shadows!

What would you like to know about shadows?
Let's think of some questions.

Tell me how could you find that out?

Planning, Years 5 and 6: Launch pad

Here is a type of lever used to open a tin.

What would you like to know about levers?

Let's think of some questions.

I want to know if …

How does where I push make a difference to the load I can lift? Tell me what to do!

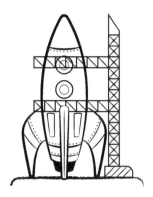

Observation, Years 3 and 4: Launch pad

What's in the school garden?

What can you see?

What are they like?

How are they different?

How are they the same?

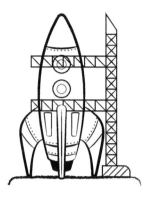

Observation, Years 3 and 4: Launch pad

Let's make some noise!

How did you make the sound?

How can you change the sound?

How do you know you changed the sound?

Observation, Years 5 and 6: Launch pad

How can we tell these fossils apart?

How are they different?

How are they the same?

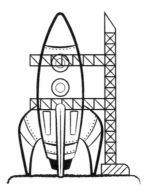

Analysing, Years 1 and 2: Launch pad

Does the root grow faster than the shoot?

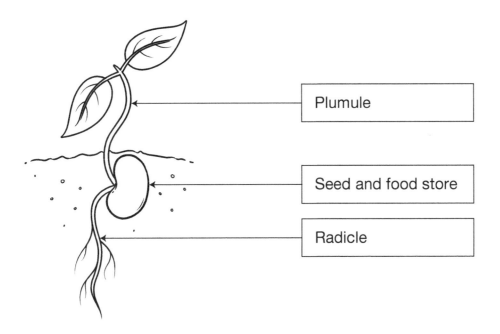

Look at the results. How do you know?

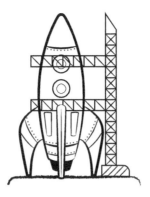

Analysing, Years 3 and 4: Launch pad

Which is the hardest rock?

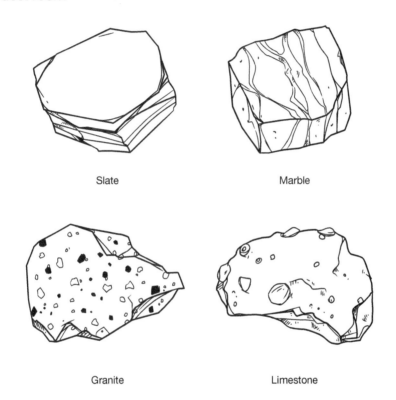

Slate

Marble

Granite

Limestone

Look at the results. How do you know?

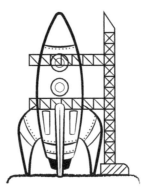

Analysing, Years 5 and 6: Launch pad

Who is the fittest in the class?

Look at the results. How do you know?

Evaluating, Years 1 and 2: Launch pad

I think woodlice are only found under rocks. I am going to count all the woodlice under rocks.

I think woodlice are found anywhere that is dark and damp. I'm going to give them a choice of dark or damp and see which one they prefer.

Who is right? Lucy or George?

What would you do?

Would you do anything differently?

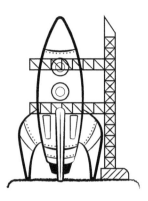

Evaluating, Years 3 and 4: Launch pad

What I did was I put three different drinks in three different beakers. One was a fizzy drink, one was water and the other was orange juice, and then I put an eggshell in them.

What I found out was the fizzy drink dissolved the eggshell. The water didn't and the orange juice decayed it a little.

What is Susie trying to find out?

Did she find it out?

Could she say for sure?

Can you think of some other questions she could answer with this investigation?

Look at what she did. Would you do anything differently?

Can you think of any ways to improve her investigation?

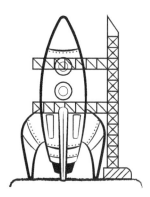

Evaluating, Years 5 and 6: Launch pad

What I did was I put some hot drink into four different types of cup: plastic, polystyrene, china and glass. I left them for 10 mins and then measured the temperature.

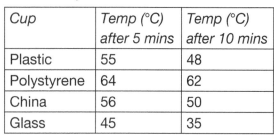

Here are my results ...

Cup	Temp (°C) after 5 mins	Temp (°C) after 10 mins
Plastic	55	48
Polystyrene	64	62
China	56	50
Glass	45	35

The polystyrene cup was warmest and the glass cup was the coldest. The other two were in between.

What is Susie trying to find out?

Did she find it out?

Could she say for sure?

Look at what she did. Would you do anything differently?

Tell her what to do to improve her investigation

Can you think of some other questions she could answer with this investigation?

Appendix 5 Support sheets

Precise and accurate observations

Using the equipment you have, make measurements of each of your fossils and record your results in the table below.

Try 1

	Fossil 1	Fossil 2	Fossil 3	Fossil 4	Fossil 5	Fossil 6
Length						
Width						
Mass						
Colour						
Texture						
Any other observation						

Try 2

	Fossil 1	Fossil 2	Fossil 3	Fossil 4	Fossil 5	Fossil 6
Length						
Width						
Mass						
Colour						
Texture						
Any other observation						

Try 3

	Fossil 1	Fossil 2	Fossil 3	Fossil 4	Fossil 5	Fossil 6
Length						
Width						
Mass						
Colour						
Texture						
Any other observation						

When compared with someone else's in my group, my observations were …

When compared with another group's, our observations were …

To make an observation more accurate …

To make an observation more precise …

Trilobites

Sam has found a fossil of an animal called a trilobite. These are animals that used to live in the sea many millions of years ago. They are very similar to crabs. There were many different types but they all followed a basic body plan like the one below.

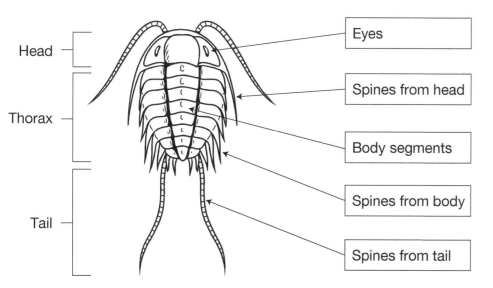

Head

Thorax

Tail

Eyes

Spines from head

Body segments

Spines from body

Spines from tail

Sam has found some more trilobites. Let's help him tell them apart.

How are the trilobites different?

What will you observe?

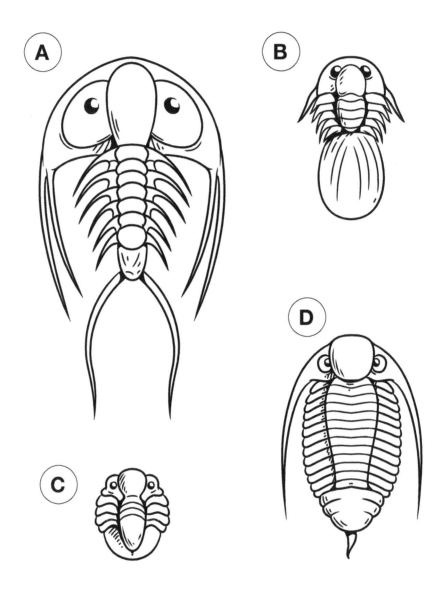

Investigating soil

Which soil does water run through fastest?

Brief method: 200ml of water was poured through a funnel containing soil. The amount of water that was collected in the measuring cylinder was measured at different times.

Type of soil	Water after 2 mins	Water after 4 mins	Water after 6 mins	Water after 8 mins	Water after 10 mins
Clay	0	2	5	10	10
Sand	25	57	100	135	185
Garden soil	10	23	35	65	95
Gravel	194	197	199	199	199
Compost	56	68	98	135	175

What are the experimenters trying to find out?

Can you answer the question?

Can you see a pattern in the results?

Can you see any results that don't fit the pattern?

Can you see any results you couldn't use?

Writing a conclusion: Investigating soils

Conclusion 1

Looking at the results I can see a clear pattern. The soils with bigger particles let the most water through and let it through in a faster time.

For example, I can see that gravel that had big particles let through 199ml of the water in 10 mins; sand, which was a bit smaller but still quite big, let through 185ml of the water in 10 mins.

The clay, which had the smallest particles (I couldn't see any just a brown blob), let through the least water (10ml in 10 mins) and it looked wet and soggy after, which meant all the water stayed in the clay.

The garden soil had a mixture of small and large particles and I expected it to be in the middle and it was. It let through 95ml in 10 mins.

The compost, which looked like garden soil but with a few bigger particles and sticks in it, let through 175ml in 10 mins so this was a bit unexpected.

I think my experiment was fair because I used the same amount of soil and the same amount of water. It was accurate because I used a measuring cylinder that measured in ml and I did all the measurements.

I could use all my results in my conclusion.

Conclusion 2

We could answer the question and the answer was gravel and sand let the most water through. We think this is because we could see large gaps between the bits of sand and gravel and this let the water through.

Conclusion 3

Looking at my results I can say for sure that sand and gravel let most water through and gravel let it through the fastest. Sand was close to the gravel. Clay was the slowest for letting water through and it also let through the least. The garden soil was in the middle. There weren't any results that didn't fit the pattern although I was a bit confused with compost as it looked more like soil and I expected it to keep more water.

I think this happens because the more soil-like (brown with little pieces) the more soil it keeps and the slower it lets water through.

Investigating pulse rates

Who has the fastest pulse rate after exercise, boys or girls?

Brief method: We looked at five boys and five girls. We took their pulse rates before exercise and then got them to do 2 mins skipping. We then took their pulse rates. We then got them to do another 2 mins skipping and took their pulse rates and then we got them to do another 2 mins exercise and took their pulse rates.

Pupil	Girl or boy	Pulse before exercise	Pulse after 2 mins exercise	Pulse after 4 mins exercise	Pulse after 6 mins exercise
1	G	65	85	100	107
2	G	57	100	110	125
3	G	72	88	65	95
4	G	56	76	92	102
5	G	68	78	95	125
6	B	68	80	95	114
7	B	56	76	92	103
8	B	70	82	100	110
9	B	95	90	105	126
10	B	60	72	98	109

What are the experimenters trying to find out?

Can you answer the question?

Can you see a pattern in the results?

Can you see any results that don't fit the pattern?

Can you see any results you couldn't use?

Writing a conclusion: Investigating pulse rate

Who has the fastest pulse rate after exercise, boys or girls?

Conclusion 1

Looking at the results, the answer to my question is neither. Both girls' and boys' pulse rates went up after exercise.

If we look at all the boys their pulse rate went up (five out of five). If we look at all the girls their pulse rate went up (five out of five).

I also looked to see if the boys' pulse rate went up higher than the girls' and there was no pattern. For example, two girls and one boy had the highest pulse rate after exercise.

There was one result that didn't fit the pattern and that was boy 9 – his pulse rate seemed to go down at first and then up again. This might mean that he didn't accurately measure his pulse rate. I don't think I can trust his result.

I think my experiment was fair because I used the same boys and girls, got them to skip for the same amount of time and got them to measure their pulses in the same place. There might have been a problem because some of the girls didn't really skip so I wouldn't have expected their pulse rate to go up that much.

I don't think my results were all that accurate because all the individuals measured their own pulse rates so they may have miscounted. They did all use stopwatches so that helped make it more accurate.

I could use all my results in my conclusion.

Conclusion 2

We could answer the question and the answer was girls as their pulse rates went up. We think this is because boys are fitter than girls so their pulse rates don't go up as much.

Conclusion 3

Looking at my results I cannot say for sure who has the fastest pulse rate as they all went up some. Girls seemed to have the lowest numbers (there was one who was lowest after exercise) so I can say they might have a slightly lower rate after exercise but I can't say for sure. I think this happens because girls are slightly fitter than boys. There were some results that didn't fit this pattern. Boy 9 seemed to start really high and then went down and then went up again. This could be because they didn't measure their pulse rate good enough.

I think our experiment was fair because we all did it at the same time and measured our pulse rates in the same way, but might not have been that fair because some girls didn't skip very hard so their pulse rates may not have gone up as much.

Investigating tooth decay

Fizzy drinks cause tooth decay.

Method
1 Measure 200ml of each liquid and put it into a glass or jar with a lid.
2 Measure out 50g of eggshell and put into each of the jars.
3 Leave the eggshell in the drink, initially overnight, and then measure the mass of the eggshell. Replace the drink.
4 Leave the eggshell in the drink for another two days and then measure the mass of the eggshell. Replace the drink.
5 Leave the eggshell in the drink for another two days and then measure the mass of the eggshell. Replace the drink.

Drink	Mass (g) before	Mass (g) after 1 day	Mass (g) after 3 days	Final mass (g) after 5 days
Fizzy water	50	50	Forgot to do it	50
Cola	50	50	47	45
Orange juice	50	50	Spilt the drink	Spilt the drink
Still water	50	50	50	50
Lemonade	40	50	48	43
Milk	50	50	50	50
Vinegar	50	46	32	10

What are the experimenters trying to find out?

Can you think of some other questions they could answer with this investigation?

Can you see any results that don't fit the pattern?

Can you see any results you couldn't use?

Would you do anything differently?

Can you think of a way to improve this investigation?

Writing an evaluation: Fizzy drinks cause tooth decay

Evaluation 1

The evidence we got was good. The reason why the evidence was good was because we checked our observations and agreed on what we saw before we wrote it down. This made our results accurate. Our evidence was quite fair because we tried to add the same amount of drink to the same amount of eggshell. The problem we found was that it was difficult to get exactly the same amount of eggshell as Susie didn't know how to work the set of scales. Some eggshell was also powdery and in little bits and floated on top of the drink.

We didn't really see a pattern except some drinks made the eggshell dissolve and others didn't.

Evaluation 2

We were trying to find out if fizzy drinks caused tooth decay. By looking at the results we couldn't say for sure if fizzy drinks caused the tooth decay. This was because the fizzy water didn't make any difference but the coke and lemonade did. We also saw that the vinegar had a really big effect on the eggshell so we can't say for sure.

The experiment went okay but Susie forgot to measure the weight of the eggshell in fizzy water on day 3 – it didn't look like it made a difference but you never know.

George also was clumsy and spilt the orange juice so we couldn't really tell if it had an effect.

We tried to make our results accurate because Susie measured the weights each time using a digital balance and this gives us a more accurate reading. We can't say our results were precise because we only did the experiments once so we don't know if we made some mistakes in our measurements.

If we were to do this investigation again, we would make sure we checked our results and then repeat the experiment. This would see if we got the same results and then we would know they were true.

I would also like to find out why some non-fizzy drinks made the eggshells decay so I would need to find out how fizzy drinks are similar or different, even though vinegar is non-fizzy.

Evaluation 3

If we were to do this experiment again we would make sure that we measured all the drinks because we left the water out.

In this experiment we worked well as a group. Me and my friends added the drink to the eggshell and wrote down what we saw.

We got results for every experiment we did and even when the eggshell did not change we noted this down as a result. The experiment was fair because we followed all the instructions and did not make any mistakes. Our results were accurate because we took lots of care to write down everything we saw.

If we were to do the experiment again we would try different fizzy drinks to see if they made the eggshell dissolve.

Investigating insulation

The diameter of the cup opening affects how long a drink stays warm.

Method

1   Get five cups of the same material but with different diameter openings.
2   Add 200ml of hot water into each cup.
3   Measure the temperature every 2 mins.
4   After 10 mins stop measuring.

Diameter of cup opening	Temp (°C) after 2 mins	Temp (°C) after 4 mins	Temp (°C) after 6 mins	Temp (°C) after 8 mins	Temp (°C) after 10 mins
5cm	60	59	Forgot to do it	56	55
7cm	58	57	57	55	54
9cm	58	57	Spilt the water and refilled it	60	59
10cm	63	55	58	53	52
11cm	56	50	55	52	48

What are the experimenters trying to find out?

Can you think of some other questions they could answer with this investigation?

Can you see any results that don't fit the pattern?

Can you see any results you couldn't use?

Would you do anything differently?

Can you think of a way to improve this investigation?

Writing an evaluation: The diameter of the cup opening affects how long a drink stays warm

Evaluation 1

The evidence we got was good. The reason why the evidence was good was because we checked our observations and agreed on what we saw before we wrote it down. This made our results accurate. Our evidence was quite fair because we tried to add the same amount of drink to all the cups. The problem we found was that it was difficult to measure the opening of the cup because Susie didn't know where to measure to and we couldn't agree.

We did kind of see a pattern but the 9cm didn't fit it.

Evaluation 2

I think we did okay. We worked hard and completed all the work. The results we got we used to answer the question and the pattern we saw was the bigger the opening the quicker the drink cooled down – this was because there was more space for the heat to escape. We kept all our cups fair so our investigation was fair. We used a thermometer and that gave us good results.

Evaluation 3

If we were to do this experiment again we would make sure that we measured all the temperatures all the time.

In this experiment we worked well as a group. Me and my friends added the water and it went down in temperature so it worked. We got results for every experiment we did. The experiment was fair because we followed all the instructions and did not make any mistakes. Our results were accurate because we took lots of care to write down everything we saw.

If we were to do the experiment again we would try different-sized cups to see if that made a difference.

We were trying to find out if the size of the opening to the cup affects how long it stays warm.

Looking at the results we could say for sure that the bigger the opening the quicker the cup cooled down. This was because all the results showed that except for the 9cm one and we didn't know what happened there.

The experiment went okay but Vimal forgot to measure the 5cm cup at 6 mins but the results continued to go down so I don't think it made much difference.

George also was clumsy and spilt the water in the 9cm and then he refilled it so this was probably why it didn't fit the pattern because the fresh water was hotter.

We tried to make our results accurate because Susie measured the temperature each time using a digital thermometer and this gives us a more accurate reading. We can't say our results were precise because we only did the experiments once, so we don't know if we made some mistakes in our measurements.

If we were to do this investigation again we would make sure we checked our results and then repeat the experiment – this would see if we got the same results and then we would know they were true.

I would like to repeat the 9cm one again especially.

I think we got accurate results that we could trust (except the 9cm one) but I would like to know if the material the cup was made from has an effect because I am sure some heat was lost through the walls of the cup.

Index